D1597702

IBM Mainframe Security:
Beyond the Basics

*A Practical Guide
from a z/OS and RACF Perspective*

Dinesh D. Dattani

MC Press Online, LLC

Boise, ID 83703 USA

IBM Mainframe Security: Beyond the Basics

A Practical Guide from a z/OS and RACF Perspective

Dinesh D. Dattani

First Edition

First Printing—August 2013

MC Press offers excellent discounts on this book when ordered in quantity for bulk purchases or special sales, which may include custom covers and content particular to your business, training goals, marketing focus, and branding interest.

Corporate Offices:
MC Press Online, LLC
3695 W. Quail Heights Court
Boise, ID 83703 3861 USA

Sales and Customer Service:
service@mcpressonline.com
(208) 629-7275 ext. 500

Permissions and Special Orders:
mcbooks@mcpressonline.com

ISBN: 978-1-58347-828-8

To my wife, Nayna,

for her unwavering support and encouragement.

Acknowledgments

When a technical book of this nature gets published, it is generally assumed that the author did all the work. Nothing could be further from the truth. In most cases there are many other individuals who have also played a role, big or small.

I would like to acknowledge the following individuals who have contributed one way or another in the publishing of this book.

First, I am grateful to Katie M. Tipton, the book editor at MC Press, for accepting my work. These days there are many potential authors all vying for the publisher's attention, and it must be hard to select from among them. As a first-time author, I consider it an honor to be offered a book-publishing contract.

I would like to thank Patrick Dzieciol. Patrick is a mainframe security colleague and author of the book *The Camp Tripper: The Secrets of Successful Family Camping in Ontario*. Patrick helped me understand various aspects of book publishing, edited parts of the manuscript, and provided many useful suggestions that I have included in the book.

I am indebted to my colleague and friend Edward Kevin Jasper. Edward reviewed and edited parts of the book as I had requested, but then went above and beyond this by offering numerous suggestions based on his extensive mainframe security experience. He also encouraged me in the book-writing effort.

Marianne Krcma, this book's copy editor, is a true professional and expert who used her vast editing experience and knowledge to transform my manuscript into the book you are reading.

My daughter, Maya Dattani, who reviewed the manuscript, did all the illustrations, and helped me understand the nuances of Microsoft® Word®.

My son, Neil D. Dattani, who edited the manuscript, offered many useful suggestions, and corrected me when I went astray.

Altaf Patel, manager of mainframe security at Royal Bank of Canada, Toronto, who reviewed the Table of Contents.

About the Author

Dinesh D. Dattani is a mainframe security consultant and president of Triple-D Mainframe Services Limited, based in Toronto, Canada. He has more than 30 years of mainframe security experience at a number of companies in North America. His consulting career spans diverse industries and sectors, including banking, telecom, automotive, insurance, energy, government, and service providers.

In addition to RACF, Dinesh has consulting experience on the mainframe security software products ACF2 and Top Secret, both from CA Technologies (formerly Computer Associates International). He has also provided hands-on and classroom training on mainframe security to a number of clients.

Before starting his own company, Dinesh was a system programmer working on mainframe operating systems. This base gave him an invaluable understanding of the technical aspects of mainframe security.

Dinesh is the author of nearly 60 articles on mainframe security, published over the past 25 years in several different journals. He is also the author of the IBM white paper *Best Practices for System z Security: Mainframe Security Matters—Thinking Outside the Box*, published and distributed by IBM in 2006. In 1996, his article "RACF Migration Experiences" was featured on the cover of the *Enterprise Systems Journal*. In 1991, he received the "Best Newsletter Article" award from the Networks and Systems Professionals Association (NaSPA) for his article "Are Mainframes Immune to Computer Viruses?"

Dinesh has a bachelor of mathematics degree with a major in computer science from the University of Waterloo, Canada.

Contents

PART TWO: SECURING THE z/OS OPERATING SYSTEM

PART THREE: SECURITY INFRASTRUCTURE MATTERS

Introduction

T ell a new university graduate that you work on mainframe security, and chances are he or she will look at you incredulously and say, "Do they *still* have mainframes?"

As in the famous quote from Mark Twain, rumors of the death of mainframes have been greatly exaggerated. Mainframes are not only alive and well; they are, in fact, the backbone of almost all IT installations in large corporations, and in many medium-sized companies, too.

About Mainframe Security

One of the strengths of the mainframe is its security. Compared to other computing platforms, mainframe security is versatile and robust. There are good reasons for this.

Mainframes have always been designed with multiple users in mind. Basic security considerations were laid out in the very foundation of the operating system, right from the start, to protect information, data, program code, and whatever else might be shared. Contrast this with the history of personal computers. Even the name "personal computer" implies that it would not be shared! These small machines were initially meant for single users only;

therefore, no thought was given to security. And so it is that in the world of personal computers, security evolved after the fact. It was added later in their evolutionary process, and only as the need arose.

There's another reason why mainframe security is miles ahead of rival platforms: personal computers were initially targeted for non-business applications, such as gaming and word processing. Mainframes, on the other hand, were built to provide financial benefits to large organizations such as financial institutions, where it would be unthinkable not to consider security from the very beginning.

Due to the superior design, performance, and stability of the mainframe system, there has been very little need to constantly update the tools and menus that accompany it. TSO, ISPF, JCL, RACF®, and other mainframe products look and feel very much the same today as they did 30 years ago. Personal computers, on the other hand, are constantly evolving, so time must be dedicated to learning their constantly changing tools and interfaces.

Lastly, the very fact that mainframes are housed behind locked doors and at nondescript locations provides a large measure of physical security. Access to them is via terminals or personal computers using secure connections such as Virtual Private Network, or VPN. Quite often, a person working on a corporation's mainframe does not even know where the physical machine is located—and does not care. This is in sharp contrast to personal computers sitting in front of you, with their ubiquitous "Ctrl-Alt-Del" shutdown provision at your fingertips. Also, most PCs come equipped with a CD or DVD drive that can potentially be used to siphon away corporate data.

This is not to say that mainframe security was always as secure as we know it today. Over time, the technology evolved, and with it, security was strengthened. The inherent benefits of mainframe security, however, are not to be taken for granted. It is left up to the installation to customize and implement many of the optional, installation-specific security features.

The proper implementation of mainframe security cannot be over-emphasized. It is vital to secure corporate assets. Auditors, both internal and external, are always on the lookout for security breaches, especially after incidents such as the Enron debacle. There are also compliance requirements, such as the

Sarbanes-Oxley Act in the United States, which mandate that adequate security and safeguards be in place to protect shareholder interests. In fact, there are even legal obligations on corporations to guard their information assets.

Mainframe security is as much about guarding business data as protecting the operating system features prone to misuse and abuse. Therefore, security practitioners must involve both application developers and system programmers to implement security. As you shall see in this book, the operating system (IBM® z/OS® or one of its predecessors, IBM OS/390® or IBM MVS™) has a number of security-related concerns that must be addressed to achieve an overall security comfort level.

About This Book

This book describes practical, real-life security issues and their solutions, gleaned from over 30 years of mainframe security experience. Wherever appropriate, quizzes are provided so you can test your knowledge with their questions and learn from their answers.

RACF, the IBM security software, is used throughout this book. Mainframe professionals who use other security software (such as ACF2 or Top Secret from CA Technologies) can also benefit from some parts of this book, as the concepts and ideas explained here apply to mainframe security in general, without regard to any particular security software.

To impart knowledge in the best way possible, the book is broken up into three major areas.

The first part focuses on how to deploy RACF properly to protect your company's business assets. RACF is, after all, just a tool to do this, and like all products that do many things, it is a complicated piece of software. Beginners to mainframe security might not appreciate all the subtle aspects of RACF. There are many levers and controls at their disposal, and using them improperly can lead not only to the inadequate protection of corporate data but even to open security "back doors" that could go unnoticed for a long time.

If RACF is complex, the z/OS operating system is even more so. It, itself, needs to be secured, and this is something many security professionals ignore.

There are two main reasons for this oversight: first, most security professionals are too busy doing daily security administration work, and second, even if they had the time, most of them do not understand the complexities of the z/OS operating system. The second part of this book, therefore, identifies the main areas of security weaknesses within the z/OS operating system and offers solutions in each case to mitigate, or close the security "gaps," as an auditor might say.

The third part of this book deals with many issues related to laying a strong security infrastructure, one that would be conducive to planting a solid security environment. Without this foundation, you cannot reap the benefits described in the other two parts of the book. The areas mentioned here must be nurtured in order to have a healthy security moat around the corporation's data.

Throughout the book, there are special sections titled, "How Secure Is *Your* Installation?" These sections will help you gauge the state of security at your installation, and strengthen it where necessary.

Who Should Read This Book

This book was written with the mainframe security practitioner in mind. However, its contents will also be useful to any IT professional who works on the mainframe platform and needs to understand its security. IT auditors will benefit by better understanding potential security weaknesses and their remedies.

The book takes the beginner beyond the basic mainframe security and RACF knowledge. For this reason, no attempt is made to explain basic RACF commands and their syntax—this information is readily available in IBM manuals. Also, basic knowledge about the mainframe, such as TSO and JCL, is assumed.

PART ONE

SECURING BUSINESS DATA

In this part, we will briefly look at how mainframe security works. We will then examine the security features and functions that RACF offers and see how these can be employed to achieve the ultimate goal of protecting all of the corporation's business assets. Security practitioners spend the bulk of their time in this endeavor.

1

How the Mainframe Provides Security

Any farmer will tell you, only a fool lets a fox guard the henhouse door.
—Proverb

One way to implement mainframe security is to let all applications running on the system manage their own security. However, that would be akin to allowing foxes to guard the henhouse. Instead,the mainframe operating system is entrusted with providing security for all users and applications sharing the computer. Being an independent entity, the operating system has no vested interest in compromising the data.

A key integrity feature of the z/OS mainframe operating system is that all programs doing work are kept apart from each other. In other words, one program cannot see what the other is doing. This segregation is implemented via a feature called *address spaces*, whereby each entity in the mainframe is allocated an address space and cannot look into other address spaces.

Thus, the very foundation of the operating system provides data integrity, as shown in Figure 1.1.

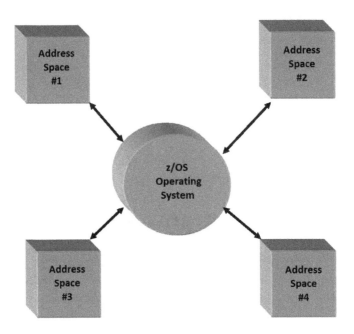

Figure 1.1: Programs are kept within their own boundaries by the operating system in the middle.

While the operating system provides basic integrity, it uses an "external" security product to do all other security checking.

When we talk about an external security product, we mean it is external to the "core" operating system. However, the security product is still part of the operating system. The security checking has been externalized from the core operating system to enable competing security products to provide mainframe security.

There are three main mainframe security products: IBM's Resource Access Control Facility, or RACF, and ACF2 and Top Secret, both from CA Technologies (formerly Computer Associates International). We will use RACF throughout this book.

The operating system intercepts all authentication and validation requests. It then passes along these requests to RACF, which in turn makes its decision based on information in its security database. In this sense, the operating system is strictly a gatekeeper or go-between; it does not actively make decisions to allow or fail the security requests.

One can think of the operating system as having subcontracted all installation-specific security checking to RACF.

How RACF Does Access Checking

When RACF receives a request for access checking, it decides to grant or deny the request based on information residing in the RACF database. RACF checking for an access request is quite involved. There are of course the "access lists" in RACF profiles that specify who has access, but that's not all. Several other factors influence RACF's decision-making process. In addition to access lists, following are the main factors RACF considers before deciding whether to grant or deny access:

1. *Universal access*—The "universal access" (UACC) specified in the profile is above and beyond what is in the access lists. For example, if the value is READ and a user ID is not in the access list, then the user ID gets at least READ access.

2. *General access*—If the profile has an entry of * (an asterisk) in its access list, all user IDs have access that is specified for *. There is a subtle difference between this general access and universal access. This is covered in chapter 11, "Security Administration: Beyond the Basics."

3. *Operations privilege*—If a user has the OPERATIONS privilege, the user might get access because of that fact. This is discussed in detail in chapter 2, "RACF Special Privileges."

4. *Global Access Checking (GAC) table*—The GAC table can grant access before the pertaining profile is even checked. This is discussed in detail in chapter 5, "The Global Access Checking (GAC) Table."

5. *RACF exits*—RACF exits can override all access definitions in the RACF database. This is discussed in detail in chapter 16, "RACF Exits."

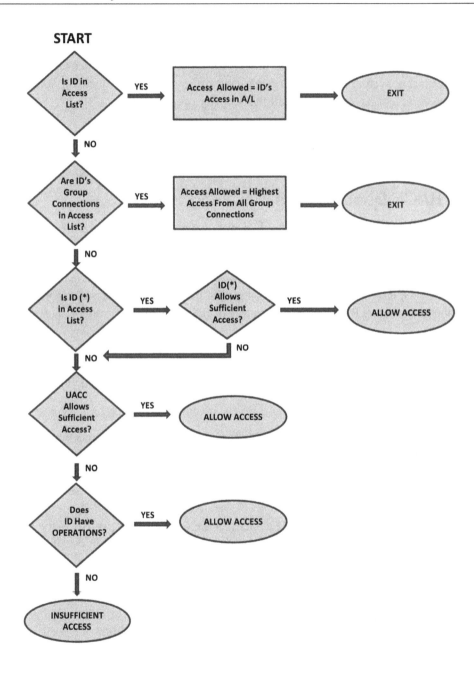

Figure 1.2: A simplified version of RACF access checking.

The RACF Access Checking Diagram

The diagram in Figure 1.2 is a simplified version of RACF authorization checking. It covers the main areas, but it does not go into the details of seldom-used cases. Let's use the diagram to understand how RACF works, by taking Quiz 1.1.

Quiz 1.1

1. The user ID JOHN is connected to two groups, GROUP01 and GROUP02. GROUP01 has READ access to the profile PROD.DATA.**, and GROUP02 has UPDATE access to the same profile. What access does JOHN have to this profile?

   Answer: JOHN will have UPDATE access, since RACF looks at accesses of all groups the user ID is connected to and grants the highest among them.

2. User ID CHAN10 is explicitly specified with READ access in the access list of the profile PROD.DATA.**, but the user ID is also connected to the group ACCT1, and ACCT1 has UPDATE access to this profile. What access does CHAN10 get, READ or UPDATE?

   Answer: In this case, the user ID will get READ access. If the user ID is explicitly mentioned in an access list, then the access specified for that user ID is always what the user ID gets, regardless of other group connections. This RACF feature comes in handy when the group is large and a few individuals in the group require less (or more) access than the others.

3. If the universal access (UACC) of a profile is UPDATE and the user ID SMITH10 is explicitly specified as having READ access, what access does the user ID get?

   Answer: SMITH10 only gets READ access. If, however, the UACC value is READ and the access list specifies UPDATE for SMITH10, then SMITH10 gets UPDATE access. In other words, the specific access overrides the universal access. This feature of RACF comes in handy when there are a few exceptions from the general access required by all users.

4. The user ID PETER6 has the powerful OPERATIONS privilege that allows full access to all of the installation's data. How can you prevent PETER6 from accessing the payroll master file?

Answer: Based on the flowchart in Figure 1.2, if a user ID is specifically mentioned in the access list, then the access specified in the access list is all the user ID gets. This is one instance where the special privilege OPERATIONS is overridden. This allows you to reduce the powers of the OPERATIONS privilege. So simply specify that user ID PETER6 is not to have any access in the access list of the profile for the payroll master file:

PERMIT 'PROFILE' ID(PETER6) ACCESS(NONE) GENERIC

2

RACF Special Privileges

In this business you don't even trust yourself.
—Former colleague

RACF has provisions for users to have special privileges. The three main special privileges are OPERATIONS, SPECIAL, and AUDITOR.

These three privileges come in two flavors: group-level and system-wide. A group-level privilege is only applicable to one RACF group, and the privilege applies only to users and resources that fall within the scope of the specified group. A system-wide privilege does not have this limitation—it applies to all resources, and to all users.

Note that the following are not discussed in this chapter:

- The UNIX® SUPERUSER privilege. For information about this privilege, refer to chapter 9, "Understanding z/OS UNIX Security."

- Special privileges available in optional system components such as DB2®, CICS®, and IMS®.

The OPERATIONS privilege allows the user to read, write, create, and delete most of the installation's data.

The SPECIAL privilege allows the user to define and administer security profiles and user IDs, and to set RACF global options through the SETROPTS command in the RACF database. It does not allow the ability to manipulate any data, although users with this privilege can do that in a roundabout way, by adding themselves to the appropriate access lists of profiles.

The AUDITOR privilege allows the holder to display all profiles in the RACF database.

In addition, your company might have other special privileges for application software, both homegrown and purchased from vendors.

Logging Special Privilege Activities

The installation should log all RACF activities that are carried out because of the special privileges of their owners. This logging is optional, so it is left up to the installation to implement it. However, auditors often want to see these logs.

Two RACF commands will turn on such logging. The first will log all activities of users carried out by virtue of their OPERATIONS or group-level OPERATIONS privilege:

```
SETROPTS OPERAUDIT
```

The other command will log all activities of users carried out by virtue of their SPECIAL or group-level SPECIAL privilege:

```
SETROPTS SAUDIT
```

Note that, if you have SAUDIT or OPERAUDIT in effect, it indicates that you want to log all accesses granted to these user IDs because of their special powers.

Other superfluous logging for these user IDs will not occur. For example, when these user IDs are in the access lists of profiles and they gain access because of that fact, that access will not be logged.

Mitigating the Risk of Special Privileges

To mitigate the risk of these special privileges, you first need to find all users having special privileges. To do this, run the Data Security Monitor (DSMON) report "Selected User Attribute Report." (DSMON reports are discussed in more detail in the next chapter.)

Here is a partial sample report:

```
        S E L E C T E D    U S E R    A T T R I B U T E    R E P O R T

   USERID   ----------------  ATTRIBUTE TYPE  ------------------------

            SPECIAL      OPERATIONS      AUDITOR      REVOKE

   --------------------------------------------------------------------

   JOHNS10  SYSTEM                       SYSTEM

   MALINDA               SYSTEM

   MARY05   SYSTEM                                    REVOKE
```

Check this report to see who has special privileges, and make sure these users need to hold special privileges.

It goes without saying that there is a great risk of special privileges being misused or abused. Auditors quite often want to know how many users are holding special privileges. You should try to minimize their use. Make sure company policy states that special privileges are handed out sparingly, and only after management approval. You should also review the logs of activities conducted by means of special privileges.

Once special privileges are handed out to a user ID or a batch ID, it is difficult to take them away. The reason? Users might not request access rights through the proper approval process, since they already have the access via special privileges.

Over time, they will be getting access to a large number of resources not through explicit and documented channels, but by means of these special privileges.

Then, when you decide to reduce the use of special privileges—possibly because of an audit finding—you will need to determine all the access rights that the user needs legitimately and grant those accesses. Only then can you remove the special privilege. Also, the person holding the special privileges might not like the idea of losing them and might try to justify having them. So, it is better not to grant these powers indiscriminately in the first place.

Here are two rules of thumb regarding special privileges:

- The AUDITOR privilege should be given only to auditors and security administrators.

- The SPECIAL privilege should be given only to security administrators and one or two batch IDs.

How about the OPERATIONS privilege? Ideally, nobody should have this very powerful privilege! There are now alternatives to using it.

The risk associated with the OPERATIONS privilege is substantial, since the holder of this privilege can not only read, but also update and delete, most (but not all) of the installation's data.

The installation can control which RACF classes are affected by the OPERATIONS privilege: for installation-defined RACF classes, you can choose whether to give special powers to holders of the OPERATIONS privilege. You specify this at the class level, in the Class Descriptor Table (CDT).

To see which RACF classes are affected at your installation, refer to the RACF Class Descriptor Table report described in the next chapter.

Alternatives to the OPERATIONS Privilege

In the past, the OPERATIONS privilege was needed so the storage administrators could manage the company's disk storage. Their job functions include backing up and migrating all data on disk, moving data between disk volumes, and so on. It would be impractical to grant them all access to all profiles. So, it was easier to make available a privilege that would achieve the same thing.

However, over the years, RACF functionality has improved. Special profiles meant specifically for the storage administration function have been introduced. These are the STGADMIN profiles in the FACILITY class. They allow storage administration-related tasks without having the OPERATIONS privilege, so the need to use the OPERATIONS privilege has diminished. (For a complete discussion on STGDMIN profiles, refer to the IBM manual *DFSMSdss Storage Administration Reference*.)

There is also a RACF class called DASDVOL that allows volume-level storage functions. Another way is to use HSM (or any storage management software you might have at your installation) to perform storage management and other "housekeeping" functions by making it a TRUSTED started procedure.

If you have user IDs that have the OPERATIONS privilege, review the activities carried out by them to see whether they can be replaced with alternatives. Your goal, of course, should be to phase out and ultimately eliminate the use of this privilege.

It is common practice, though, to allow the use of the OPERATIONS privilege on an exceptional basis, such as during disaster recovery exercises and during system emergencies. At these times, typically systems programmers and storage administrators would need special privileges.

Summary

All RACF special privileges, if misused, allow unauthorized access to the installation's data and can create a number of audit issues. So, ensure that you hand out special privileges judiciously in the first place.

✓ How Secure Is *Your* Installation?

Use the DSMON report to count the number of user IDs at your installation having the OPERATIONS privilege. Why do they need this? Are they storage administrators? If so, why are they not using alternatives to the OPERATIONS privilege?

3

The Data Security Monitor (DSMON)

Y ou'll certainly want to know whether there are any security weaknesses at your installation. How to find out?

The Data Security Monitor (DSMON) is a program that comes with RACF. DSMON produces a set of reports that identify security weaknesses (or strengths) at your installation.

A word of caution here: DSMON does not cover all aspects of mainframe security. Therefore, it should be used in conjunction with other reports and other processes. If you rely solely on DSMON reports, potential security weaknesses at your installation might go undetected.

Auditors often ask for all or specific DSMON reports. RACF security practitioners, therefore, need to know how to run and interpret these reports. You should run DSMON reports regularly to make sure no potential security exposures are creeping in, and to familiarize yourself with their contents.

How to Produce DSMON Reports

Since DSMON reports contain sensitive information, not anyone can run the DSMON program—you need the RACF AUDITOR privilege.

DSMON produces a set of ten reports. You have the choice of running all the reports or just a subset of them.

The JCL in Figure 3.1 will produce all ten reports. To produce individual reports, the line FUNCTION ALL needs to be replaced, as discussed in the following pages. (For more information about DSMON, refer to the IBM manual *z/OS Security Server RACF Auditor's Guide*.)

```
//DSMONRPT  JOB

//STEP1     EXEC PGM=ICHDSM00

//SYSPRINT  DD    SYSOUT=*

//SYSUT2    DD    SYSOUT=*

//SYSIN     DD    *

LINECOUNT 55

FUNCTION ALL
```

Figure 3.1: This JCL will produce all ten DSMON reports. Change the JOB statement to conform to your installation's standards.

Understanding DSMON Reports

All DSMON reports are important. However, some reports have more relevance than others. The reports that follow are arranged roughly in the order of their importance. In addition, some of the more important reports are covered in greater detail elsewhere in this book. Refer to the chapters indicated below for a more complete discussion of them.

The Selected User Attribute Report

To produce only the Selected User Attribute report, replace the last line of the JCL in Figure 3.1 with this:

```
FUNCTION RACUSR
```

The Selected User Attribute report shows user IDs that possess the SPECIAL, OPERATIONS, and AUDITOR attributes. This report tells you whether the attribute is system-wide or at the group level. User IDs having system-wide privileges are more of a security issue than those that have only group-level privileges. Additionally, the report shows user IDs that have been revoked. This can be used to remove (delete) inactive user IDs.

For a sample report and a complete discussion of special privileges, refer to chapter 2, "RACF Special Privileges." For a complete discussion of inactive user IDs, refer to chapter 29, "Security Best Practices."

The Selected Data Sets Report

The Selected Data Sets report lists several important operating system data sets that are defined at your installation. These include APF-authorized libraries, linklist libraries, the RACF databases, and system catalogs. For each of these data sets, the report indicates whether there is RACF protection and what the universal access (UACC) is.

To obtain individual reports for each category, do the following:

1. To get the report on linklist libraries, replace the last line in the JCL in Figure 3.1 with this:

```
FUNCTION SYSLNK
```

Note that some linklist libraries may be APF-authorized. For a sample report and a complete discussion of this topic, refer to chapter 12, "APF-Authorized Libraries."

2. To get the report on APF-authorized libraries, replace the last line in Figure 3.1 with this:

```
FUNCTION SYSAPF
```

A sample report and complete discussion of this topic is also in chapter 12.

3. To get the report on system catalogs, replace the last line in Figure 3.1 with this:

```
FUNCTION SYSCAT
```

For a sample report and a complete discussion of this topic, refer to the discussion of system catalogs in chapter 14, "Operating System Data Sets."

4. To get a report on RACF databases, replace the last line in Figure 3.1 with this:

```
FUNCTION RACDST
```

For a sample report and a complete discussion of this topic, refer to chapter 15, "RACF Databases."

5. To get the report on selected operating system data sets, replace the last line in Figure 3.1 with this:

```
FUNCTION SYSSDS
```

For a sample report and a complete discussion of this topic, refer to chapter 14.

The RACF Global Access Table Report

To produce only the Global Access Table report, replace the last line in Figure 3.1 with this:

```
FUNCTION RACGAC
```

The Global Access Table report shows classes that are activated for global access checking. A typical class that has been activated for global access checking is the DATASET class, but there may be others. The report also shows, for each active class, the profiles eligible for global access checking, together with the level of access allowed. Entries in this table are checked before a check is done in the RACF database. If access is allowed in the global access table, the RACF database check is bypassed.

For a sample report and a complete discussion of this topic, refer to chapter 5, "The Global Access Checking (GAC) Table."

The RACF Started Procedures Table Reports

To produce only the Started Procedures Table reports, replace the last line in Figure 3.1 with this:

```
FUNCTION RACSPT
```

The Started Procedures Table reports show all the started procedures at your installation. One report shows all the profiles defined in the STARTED class, and the other report shows entries in the ICHRIN03 module. The reports show special attributes assigned, if any, to each started procedure, PRIVILEGED or TRUSTED.

For a sample report and a complete discussion of this topic, refer to chapter 18, "Started Procedures."

The RACF Class Descriptor Table Report

To produce only the Class Descriptor Table report, replace the last line in Figure 3.1 with this:

```
FUNCTION RACCDT
```

The Class Descriptor Table report shows all the resource classes defined at your installation. For each resource class, it provides information such as whether the class is active, the default universal access for the class, and whether there is auditing turned on for the class.

Sample Report

Here is a sample (partial) Class Descriptor Table report:

```
R A C F    C L A S S    D E S C R I P T O R    T A B L E    R E P O R T

  CLASS                                         DEFAULT    OPERATIONS

  NAME      STATUS     AUDITING   STATISTICS    UACC       ALLOWED

  --------------------------------------------------------------------

  RVARSMBR  INACTIVE   NO         NO            NONE       NO

  RACFVARS  INACTIVE   NO         NO            NONE       NO

  SECLABEL  INACTIVE   NO         NO            NONE       NO

  DASDVOL   ACTIVE     NO         NO            ACEE       YES

  TAPEVOL   ACTIVE     NO         NO            ACEE       YES

  . . .

  . . .
```

What to Look For in This Report

Use this report to verify that resource classes that should be active are indeed
active. Quite often, someone with special powers inactivates a resource
class for some testing and forgets to reactivate it. If the class isn't one of the
important ones, this mistake might go unnoticed, but you will catch it by
reviewing this report. You can also use this report to review your audit options
for each class.

In the report, you should also review the default universal access (UACC)
in effect for each class. This default will apply whenever you don't specify a
default universal access level explicitly in any profile that you might create for
this class.

The RACF Exits Report

To produce only the RACF Exits report, replace the last line in Figure 3.1 with this:

```
FUNCTION RACEXT
```

The RACF Exits report shows RACF exits that are active at your installation. It also shows the module length (size) of each exit. For a sample report and a complete discussion of this topic, refer to chapter 16, "RACF Exits."

The Program Properties Table Report

To produce only the Program Properties Table report, replace the last line in Figure 3.1 with this:

```
FUNCTION SYSPPT
```

The Program Properties Table, or PPT for short, is a z/OS operating system module that contains mostly operating system programs capable of bypassing RACF security. The table is typically maintained by the z/OS system programmers. For a sample report and a complete discussion of this topic, refer to chapter 22, "The Program Properties Table (PPT)."

The RACF Authorized Caller Table Report

To produce only the Authorized Caller Table report, replace the last line in Figure 3.1 with this:

```
FUNCTION RACAUT
```

The Authorized Caller Table report shows programs that can make RACF calls in an authorized state, and thus change critical RACF control blocks (for example, the ACEE). For a more complete discussion of authorized programs, refer to chapter 12, "APF-Authorized Libraries."

Sample Report

Here is a partial sample Authorized Caller Table report:

```
R A C F   A U T H O R I Z E D   C A L L E R   T A B L E   R E P O R T

      MODULE            RACINIT        RACLIST

      NAME              AUTHORIZED     AUTHORIZED


      ---------------------------------------------------------------

      NO ENTRIES IN RACF AUTHORIZED CALLER TABLE
```

What to Look For in This Report

Normally, there shouldn't be any entries in this table. When you install RACF, there are usually no entries in this table. If you see any entries, you should contact your system programmers to find out whether the entries are legitimate.

The System Report

To produce only the System report, replace the last line in Figure 3.1 with this:

```
FUNCTION SYSTEM
```

As the name implies, the System report provides information related to the operating system environment, such as the CPU-ID, model, RACF version and release, and whether RACF is active in the system.

Sample Report

Here is a partial sample System report:

```
                        S Y S T E M    R E P O R T

--------------------------------------------------------------------

    CPU-ID                    123456

    CPU MODEL                 2345

    OPERATING SYSTEM/LEVEL    z/OS 1.5.2

    SYSTEM RESIDENCE VOLUME   SYSRES
```

What to Look For in This Report

When you need to know system-specific information such as the RACF release level you're running, this report is a good place to find it. In the case of multiple RACF databases, and after a RACF release upgrade, you should make sure you're running the right version of RACF.

The Group Tree Report

To produce only the Group Tree report, replace the last line in Figure 3.1 with this:

```
FUNCTION RACGRP
```

The Group Tree report shows how your RACF group structure looks. It shows all RACF groups that are defined at your installation and shows relationships among superior groups and their sub-groups. This report is not easy to read. It typically runs several pages, and there are no graphics.

Sample Report

Here is a partial sample Group Tree report:

```
              R A C F     G R O U P     T R E E     R E P O R T

LEVEL   GROUP     (OWNER

-----------------------------------------------------------------

    1   SYS1      (ADMIN1 )

        |

    2   | SYSPROG    (ADMIN1 )

        |

    2   | APPLGRP    (ADMIN2 )
```

What to Look For in This Report

You can use this report to get the overall view of your group structure.

If you're giving group-level special privileges such as SPECIAL or OPERATIONS, this report will give you an idea of what this means in terms of security administration. Also, you might be surprised to find groups (or sub-groups) that are no longer valid, in which case you might want to initiate a small project to remove them.

Summary

The DSMON reports provide a wealth of important information about the state of your installation's security. You should review them periodically to make sure there are no surprises. Remember, however, that they do not address all security areas.

4

Security Event Logging and Auditing

No government can be long secure without a formidable opposition.
—Benjamin Disraeli

Even though logging has so many useful purposes, it is optional in RACF. It is up to the organization to implement as much or as little logging as it desires.

In RACF, when we talk about logging activities, we mean auditing them. The idea behind referring to logging as auditing is that, if an event or activity is logged, it can be easily audited, if necessary. In this chapter, we use the terms "logging" and "auditing" interchangeably. (The logging and auditing of z/OS UNIX security events is discussed in chapter 9, "Understanding z/OS UNIX Security.")

There are several reasons why an installation might want to turn on the various logging options:

- Auditors often request "proofs" or even actual audit trails to prove that sensitive resources are properly guarded.

- There might be legal requirements to log certain activities.

- Various compliance legislations might mandate logging and auditing.

- The installation's internal security policy and standards might require auditing.

- Reporting on security activities can only be accomplished if there are logs and audit trails.

- An installation might need to monitor certain security events on an ongoing basis.

On z/OS mainframes, logging of security records is done to the operating system data sets called System Management Facility, or SMF, data sets. SMF data comprises not only RACF loggings, but various other system activity loggings as well. RACF logging in SMF is separated from these other loggings by the *type* of SMF records that are generated.

Typically, SMF data (and therefore RACF loggings) are retained at an installation for many years, so you can always go back and trace some event or activity that occurred in the past. You have considerable freedom in choosing what RACF activities and events you want audited, and which ones to ignore. If you change your mind, it is easy to stop what was audited before, or vice versa. For more information about SMF, refer to chapter 13, "The System Management Facility (SMF)."

Be sure to choose your auditing options carefully. Too much auditing often means that you do not have the time to review the audit reports in a meaningful way, and important events might go unnoticed. If you do too little auditing, you run the risk of missing important security activities that you will never be able to trace if the need arises.

Some of the RACF auditing activities, especially those related to violations and warnings, are also seen in the system log and on the operator console in "real time," that is, as they occur.

The rest of this chapter discusses the various auditing options available in RACF.

Auditing User Activity

If you want to audit and monitor all the activities of a user, you can assign the UAUDIT attribute to the person's user ID. This will log all data sets and other resources the user references, and all the RACF commands the user enters. The logging will be in effect until you remove the UAUDIT attribute from the user profile.

The only concern with using the UAUDIT attribute is that it will log not only violations, but successful accesses as well. This tends to generate a large amount of logging records and in most cases does not serve a useful purpose. Therefore, UAUDIT should be used sparingly.

The UAUDIT attribute is meant to be used when you suspect a user of unauthorized activities. On rare occasions it is also used for tracing or debugging purposes, when a user experiences unusual problems.

Note: UAUDIT should *not* be used to log all the activities of users with special privileges such as OPERATIONS and SPECIAL. There are other ways to do this, as discussed later in this chapter in the section "Auditing Users with Special Privileges."

Auditing Resources at the Profile Level

Auditing resources at the profile level logs accesses to the various data sets and other resources covered by the profiles. There are many options. The commands to create new profiles (ADDSD and RDEFINE) have the AUDIT keyword that allows you to make your choices. After you have created the profiles, you can change the audit specifications by using the ALTER versions of these commands (ALTDSD and RALTER).

You can indicate, for each profile, whether you want to log successful accesses, failures, or both. To see what kind of logging is in effect for a profile, you can list the profile.

In general, you only want to log successful accesses for those profiles that cover highly sensitive data. Overuse of successful auditing will generate a lot of loggings and will needlessly clutter your RACF reports.

Using the GLOBALAUDIT Operand

Like the AUDIT specification, GLOBALAUDIT also applies to individual profiles in the DATASET and general resource classes. The command syntax for GLOBALAUDIT is also very similar to that of AUDIT. The difference is that GLOBALAUDIT is meant for auditors (who have the AUDITOR attribute or the GROUP-AUDITOR attribute).

Auditors can, using GLOBALAUDIT, *increase* the amount of logging for data set and general resource profiles, as specified in the AUDIT operand. They cannot, however, decrease the loggings specified in the AUDIT specification. For example, suppose a data set profile has the following specification:

```
AUDIT(FAILURES(UPDATE))
```

It indicates logging of all violations for UPDATE, CONTROL, and ALTER, but not for READ. An auditor might also wish to log violations at the READ level, so he or she can specify this:

```
GLOBALAUDIT(FAILURES(READ))
```

When you list a data set profile or a general resource profile, you see both specifications, AUDIT and GLOBALAUDIT, for that profile.

Auditing Resources at the Class Level

In addition to auditing resources at the profile level, RACF provides for audit specifications at the class level. This can be helpful in cases where you want to treat all auditing for a specific RACF class uniformly. Class-level auditing also ensures that activities deemed important will be logged, regardless of what audit options are specified in the profiles themselves.

In general, the options you specify at the global level, using the SETROPTS command, are more important than the specifications in the profiles themselves.

For class-level auditing, use the LOGOPTIONS keyword of the SETROPTS command. Class-level auditing can supersede any auditing specification you might have at the profile level in that class.

The following command will log all activity to all data set accesses, even though the data set profiles might say otherwise:

```
SETROPTS LOGOPTIONS(ALWAYS(DATASET))
```

The following command will turn off auditing for accesses to all data sets:

```
SETROPTS LOGOPTIONS(NEVER(DATASET))
```

Needless to say, this is dangerous, and is not recommended!

Here is a small exercise to make sure you do not have any RACF classes where logging has been turned off completely. Enter the following command:

```
SETROPTS LIST
```

See if you have any classes with the LOGOPTIONS: NEVER specification. If you do, make sure the setting is justified.

The following command will log all successful accesses to all data sets:

```
SETROPTS LOGOPTIONS(SUCCESSES(DATASET))
```

Successes will be logged *in addition* to what is already specified in the individual profiles.

The following command will log all failures to data set accesses:

```
SETROPTS LOGOPTIONS(FAILURES(DATASET))
```

Again, failures will be logged in addition to what is already specified in the individual profiles. This specification is highly recommended for all your important classes, in case the logging of failures is missing in some of the profiles.

The following command will honor the audit specifications in the profiles:

```
SETROPTS LOGOPTIONS(DEFAULT(DATASET))
```

This is also the default specification if you do not specify one of the above LOGOPTIONS keywords.

Auditing Users with Special Privileges

The activities of users having either the SPECIAL or OPERATIONS attribute should be logged. However, you should only log those activities that are carried out as a result of their special privileges. For more information about this topic, refer to chapter 2, "RACF Special Privileges."

Auditing Profile Changes

You might wish to log changes to all profiles, by RACF commands such as ADDSD and ALTDSD. This is not to be confused with auditing resource accesses protected by the profiles, discussed earlier in this chapter in the section "Auditing Resources at the Profile Level."

If you want to log changes made to profiles, do so on a class-by-class basis, with this command:

```
SETROPTS AUDIT(DATASET)
```

This will record changes made to profiles in the DATASET class. Other valid class names are any of the general resource classes at your installation, or USER, or GROUP.

If you specify the following, you will see changes made to all profiles in all classes at your installation:

| SETROPTS AUDIT(*) |

This is recommended, and it has the added benefit that if you were to activate a new RACF class, the new class would automatically be covered by this specification. Note that the default for this option is NOAUDIT(*), so no logging occurs for any of the classes unless you take specific action.

Auditing Failures to RACF Commands

Just as you want to see violations for accesses to data sets and other resources, you might want to see all failures to RACF commands themselves. You can audit all violations to RACF commands by specifying the following command:

| SETROPTS CMDVIOL |

This command will ignore violations caused to the "list-type" commands, such as LISTUSER, but will report all other violations to RACF commands. For example, it will report violations that occur because a user is not authorized to modify a particular profile.

RACF Automatic Loggings

RACF automatically logs some security activities. For example, if the PROTECTALL(FAILURES) option is in effect at your installation and a user with the SPECIAL privilege (or a started procedure with the TRUSTED or the PRIVILEGED attribute) requests access to an unprotected data set, RACF will grant the access, but will also always log this event, and will issue a warning message to the operator console. RACF also automatically logs all accesses granted to a resource by virtue of the profile being in WARNING mode.

The Importance of Security Log Retention

Most installations retain SMF records for several years. If yours is not doing this, it is strongly recommended that you do so.

Even if you are retaining SMF records (and therefore RACF logging activities) for long periods, it is highly recommended that you separate the security loggings from SMF on a daily, weekly, monthly, and even yearly basis. That way, if you ever need to go back and trace some RACF activity, you will not have to rely on the general SMF records.

Quiz 4.1

1. User ID JOHN05 tries to read a data set. RACF fails the access attempt, but the failure is not reported in the system log—there were no ICH*nnnn* messages indicating there was a RACF violation on the profile covering the data set. What is happening?

   Answer: The most likely explanation is that the profile covering the data set might have the auditing specification:

   AUDIT(ALL(NONE))

   This says that auditing is not required for successful accesses, or for access failures. To see these failures in the system log, you need to change the audit specification. Enter the following command:

   ALTDSD 'YOUR.DATASET.PROFILE' AUDIT(FAILURES(READ))

2. A data set profile has the following audit specification:

   AUDIT(FAILURES(UPDATE))

   If a user tries to READ a data set covered by this profile, and fails, will this event be logged?

   Answer: No, it will not be logged. Audit specifications do not "percolate" downwards—they percolate upwards. This specification says that you want to audit all failures at the UPDATE level and above, so failures for UPDATE, CONTROL, and ALTER will be logged, but READ will not be logged.

   The confusion arises because access *rights* do percolate downwards. For example, users who have UPDATE access will automatically have READ access, as well.

Summary

RACF provides many auditing options. This is one of the strengths of IBM mainframes. However, you have to choose the correct settings for your organization and implement them. This task takes time and effort, but in the end it is worth it. Unfortunately, not all companies expend the necessary effort to do this.

✓ How Secure Is *Your* Installation?

Enter the SETROPTS LIST command and look at the audit options specified at your installation. Are they in line with your company's business requirements? If any active RACF class is not being audited, what is the rationale for this?

5

The Global Access Checking (GAC) Table

Many beginners to RACF are not aware of the existence of the Global Access Checking (GAC) table. They might not realize that this table has implications for how they perform their daily security administration duties.

The GAC table consists of RACF profile entries. These entries can belong to the DATASET class, or to any of the general resource classes that are active at your installation. You can specify, for each entry in the table, the level of access to be provided, such as READ or UPDATE.

When an access request is made, RACF checks the GAC table before it checks the profiles in the RACF database. If RACF finds a match, it grants the requestor access to the resource without even checking the actual profile in the database. In effect, GAC entries override RACF profiles whenever there is a match. The only exception to this is when the user ID has the RESTRICTED attribute. In this case, GAC processing is ignored.

An important point to keep in mind is that the GAC table only grants access; it can never deny access to a resource. In other words, during GAC checking, if a profile match is not found, then RACF continues further processing by checking the RACF database, before failing (or granting) access.

Although GAC applies to any resource class, most installations use it for the DATASET class only.

The Benefits of GAC

The main benefit of the GAC table is that it speeds up RACF processing. The GAC table is in main memory, so if it is determined that access is to be granted, a lot of time is saved by not checking the RACF database itself. In computer processing terms, this is a huge performance benefit. Apart from this benefit, it does not provide additional security, nor does it make your installation more secure.

Another benefit is that you need to set up proper GAC entries only once. After that, all you need is a periodic review. You will reap the rewards every day, though!

GAC is a useful feature, and you can use it to your advantage by understanding its powers and capabilities. Used properly, it has the potential to simplify and enhance security administration.

The Security Concerns of GAC

If the GAC table is not used properly, you can introduce security exposures in your environment.

For example, if you are unaware how GAC processing works, you might simply look at a RACF profile and think you have adequately protected the underlying resources. In fact, the GAC table might have an entry for that resource that allows everyone access. The GAC table would, in effect, become a wide-open back door through which anyone could walk, while you have taken precautions to guard your front door by building appropriate RACF profiles.

A related concern about GAC is best explained with an example. Suppose you have this entry in the GAC table:

```
SYS1.**/READ
```

This allows READ access to everybody without checking any RACF profiles.

Now let's say that during the course of an audit, the auditors point out that SYS1.PARMLIB should not be read by everybody. So you create a profile SYS1.PARMLIB and make its universal access NONE, expecting this to satisfy audit concerns.

However, you might have forgotten that long ago you set up your GAC table to allow READ access to everyone to all data sets starting with SYS1! The result is that when anyone tries to read SYS1.PARMLIB, RACF does not even bother to check your newly created profile for SYS1.PARMLIB. It checks the GAC table, and since that allows access, no further checks are made.

Such are the intricacies of the GAC table.

Another important point to keep in mind is that if access is granted via GAC, then there is no logging in SMF, even if you have specified auditing specifications in the "mirror profile" (discussed later in this chapter). Only use GAC when you do not need SMF logging. Since GAC only allows access, and never denies it, the case for logging is somewhat mitigated, because the need to log successes is very little, especially for non-sensitive resources.

Implementing GAC

To implement GAC processing, you need to activate the GLOBAL class. This is a RACF class like any other. Enter the following command:

```
SETROPTS CLASSACT(GLOBAL)
```

Once you have the GLOBAL class active, you can selectively use it for GAC processing. If, for example, you only want to turn it on for the DATASET class, you issue these commands:

```
SETROPTS GLOBAL(DATASET)
```

```
RDEFINE GLOBAL DATASET
```

Then, add entries for the DATASET class. The following command will provide UPDATE access to everyone to the SYS1.BRODCAST data set:

```
RALTER GLOBAL DATASET ADDMEM('SYS1.BRODCAST'/UPDATE)
```

To remove the same entry, enter this command:

```
RALTER GLOBAL DATASET DELMEM('SYS1.BRODCAST'/UPDATE)
```

After each change to the GLOBAL class, you need to do a refresh to effect the change. For example, for the DATASET class, enter this command:

```
SETROPTS REFRESH GLOBAL(DATASET)
```

Mitigating the Security Risks of GAC

You should create entries in the GAC table for non-sensitive resources only—that is, those resources that everyone should access anyway.

To find out whether your GAC table has any security risks, first find out what has been specified in the GLOBAL class. There are several ways to do this:

- You can run the DSMON report labeled "RACF Global Access Table Report." A partial sample report appears on the following page:

```
R A C F     G L O B A L     A C C E S S     T A B L E     R E P O R T

    CLASS               ACCESS          ENTRY

    NAME                LEVEL           NAME

------------------------------------------------------------------------

    DATASET             READ            ISPF.**

    DATASET             UPDATE          SYS1.BRODCAST
```

For information about this DSMON report, refer to chapter 3, "The Data Security Monitor (DSMON)."

- You can use the RLIST command:

RLIST GLOBAL DATASET

You can substitute any other RACF class for DATASET.

- You can use the SEARCH command:

SEARCH CLASS(GLOBAL)

Once you know what is in your GAC table, make sure each resource entry is for non-sensitive data. Also make sure the entry is for a profile that is likely to be used frequently. Otherwise, there is not much benefit to putting it in the GAC table.

Next, create mirror profiles for each entry in the GAC table. A mirror profile mirrors the GAC entry in an actual RACF profile.

It is highly recommended that you create mirror profiles for all entries in the GAC table. This is where you define a "real" RACF profile for every entry in the GAC table.

For example, suppose you have this entry in the GAC table:

> SYS1.BRODCAST/UPDATE

You should define the following RACF profile:

> ADDSD 'SYS1.BRODCAST' UACC(UPDATE) GENERIC DATA('Mirror profile for GAC entry')

The installation data field will help you remember there is a corresponding entry in the GAC table.

The Benefits of GAC Mirror Profiles

The mirror profiles will not be accessed by RACF access checking. Yet, there are several benefits to creating them:

- It becomes easier to see whether someone has access just by listing profiles and not having to worry about GAC overriding any access.

- If you want to make changes to a profile that is also in the GAC table, you become aware of the implications of making your change.

- Mirror profiles are useful for auditing purposes. Auditors often look for mirror profiles for entries in the GAC table.

- If for some reason the GLOBAL class becomes inactive—and some day it might, even by mistake—then you will have something to fall back on. The mirror profiles will take over and provide equivalent access. You will not have security violations and failures.

You must, of course, remember to keep the mirror profiles in synch with the GAC entries. If you make changes to mirror profiles, remember to update the GAC also, if it is appropriate. Similarly, any changes to GAC should be reflected in the mirror profiles.

Quiz 5.1

1. A user is getting access to a profile, even though the user ID is not in the access list of the profile, nor is it connected to any groups in the access list. The universal access of the profile is NONE, and the user ID does not have OPERATIONS privilege. Why (or how) is the user getting access?

   Answer: It is possible the GAC table is allowing the access.

2. User ID PATEL20 is trying to access a data set. The GAC table specifies ALTER access to the profile covering the data set, but the access list for this profile specifies only READ access for the user ID. What access does PATEL20 get?

   Answer: The user ID gets ALTER access, since GAC supersedes the profile.

Finally, if you do not implement mirror profiles, you might have confusing situations, such as those described in quiz 5.1. In both of the quiz questions, the answers would have been obvious if you had mirror profiles.

Good Candidates for GAC Processing

Good candidates for GAC processing are resources that meet these criteria:

- The resource is non-sensitive.

- Everyone at your installation needs to access the resource.

- The resource is frequently accessed. Since the benefits of GAC are performance-related, it doesn't make sense to put in entries that are not frequently used.

To find such candidates at your installation, you will have to do some research. Each installation has its own unique naming standards and requirements. However, there are some candidates that are applicable to all installations. The following are good candidates for GAC processing in the DATASET class:

- SYS1.BRODCAST/UPDATE

- SYS1.HELP/READ

- SYS1.PROCLIB/READ

- ISPF.**/READ

- CATALOG.**/READ

- &RACUID.**/ALTER

By adding these resources to the GAC table, you will greatly speed up your RACF processing. However, first make sure they are in line with your company's standards and policies.

The last entry is worth noting. It says that, if the data set's high-level qualifier starts with the person's user ID, allow full (ALTER) access to that person, without any RACF profile checking! This specification has wide-ranging implications: it allows all TSO users complete control over their own TSO data sets. You avoid having to create profiles for each TSO user ID, resulting in considerable savings in administration effort, and also in RACF processing. Note that this is one instance where you might not want to create mirror profiles!

Apart from the above list, there might be other candidates at your installation, based on unique needs.

You should periodically review all GAC entries to make sure they are still valid, and to ensure there are mirror profiles for each entry.

Summary

If you are not using GAC processing at your installation, you might be missing out on some of its benefits. If you are using it, make sure you have not left any security "back doors" wide open.

✓ How Secure Is *Your* Installation?

If your GAC table allows UPDATE, CONTROL, or ALTER access to "masked" data set entries, you need to review them for appropriateness.

Here are two examples of inappropriate entries:

* HLQ.**/UPDATE

* HLQ.**.DATA/ALTER

The entry &RACUID.**/ALTER is an exception and may be used if you choose to do so.

6

Understanding the FACILITY Class

The RACF general resource class called FACILITY is different from other general resource classes. While other classes protect one specific area, or one specific type of resource, this one protects a miscellaneous and assorted group of resources that do not have anything in common, or those that do not fit in anywhere else. In this sense, it is a class meant for assorted security requirements. It might as well have been named the "miscellaneous" or "assorted" class.

The need for such a miscellaneous class clearly exists. Before the FACILITY class was introduced, some companies used the DATASET class, with pseudo data set names, to do RACF checking for home-grown applications. This obviously was a roundabout way of doing things, and while it accomplished the security goal, the method was hard to understand for beginning security practitioners. It was not appealing from an audit perspective, either.

The FACILITY class provides, among other things, security controls for functions and resources in the z/OS operating system such as storage management and RACF.

Although many of the services protected by the FACILITY class are operating system-type resources, conceptually you can implement protection for any resources, including home-grown ones. In addition, your installation might even have outside, non-IBM software vendors that use this class to provide security for their products.

Essentially, when a new software product is developed and security is required, the developers have to decide whether to introduce a whole new RACF class or to utilize the FACILITY class. The answer will depend upon such factors as how large the product is, how many profiles there are going to be, how often they will be used, and so on.

Some examples will help illustrate the diverse nature of the FACILITY class. These examples are limited to IBM-supplied software products only.

Storage Administration Profiles

The protection of storage management functions in z/OS is done through profiles in the FACILITY class. These profiles begin with STGADMIN. Storage management has many functions, and each needs to be segregated. So the second qualifier of these profiles further narrows down the specific storage management software product being protected. Here are several examples:

- STGADMIN.ADR.** profiles protect DFDSS functions.

- STGADMIN.IDC.** profiles protect IDCAMS functions.

- STGADMIN.IGD.** profiles protect SMS functions.

- STGADMIN.ARC.** profiles protect DFHSM functions.

z/OS UNIX Profiles

All z/OS UNIX profiles begin with BPX. These profiles are discussed in more detail in chapter 9, "Understanding z/OS UNIX Security."

RACF Profiles

RACF itself needs to control the use of some of its functions. This is done via profiles in the FACILITY class. These profiles begin with IRR.

Here are two examples of RACF profiles in the FACILITY class:

- The profile IRR.LISTUSER specifies who can list user IDs without having special privileges such as SPECIAL or AUDITOR.

- The profile IRR.PASSWORD.RESET grants permission to reset user ID passwords only. This profile is the ideal way to transfer the password-reset functions to the Help Desk, for example. That way, you do not have to give powerful privileges such as SPECIAL or even GROUP-SPECIAL to the Help Desk staff.

Other Profiles

There are many more profiles. For example, the ICHBLP profile provides the Bypass Label Processing (BLP) capability. The Distributed Computing Environment (DCE) also uses profiles in this class. In the future, there might very well be other profiles introduced in the FACILITY class.

Security Administration of FACILITY Class Profiles

As you have seen, there is a wide range of profiles in this class. Administering them is not easy. To properly administer them, a security practitioner would need to have background knowledge of a number of software products.

One option is to decentralize the security administration of these profiles. This allows you to delegate some of the administration duties to the people who are closer to the function or feature being protected, and who are therefore more qualified to make decisions on access requirements. For example, the z/OS UNIX group can be delegated the task of administering profiles that belong to z/OS UNIX (those beginning with BPX). Similarly, the Storage Administration group can administer their profiles (those beginning with STGADMIN).

If your installation has a policy of not decentralizing the security function, then another alternative is to work closely with other groups (UNIX, Storage Management, and so on) for setting up security controls.

In either case, the security department still needs to have overall control of the FACILITY class. This can be done by adequately auditing the FACILITY class. (For more information, refer to chapter 4, "Security Event Logging and Auditing.")

The FACILITY Class's Documentation

The security administrator might well wonder, where are the FACILITY class profiles documented? Because of their widely diverse use, there is no single place! You might have to refer to several different places. The *RACF Security Administrator's Guide* is a good starting point. It has a section called "Planning for Profiles in the FACILITY Class."

Third-Party Vendor Products

Third-party vendor products are those that are not from IBM. OMEGAMON®, the z/OS system performance monitor, is a good example of a third-party product.

If your company is installing a third-party software product and security for the product falls under the FACILITY class, you need to ensure that the profile names are in line with your standards and that they do not conflict with existing profile names. A good way to do this is to make sure the vendor's product name is part of the profile description.

In-House Developed Products

Some installations develop their own software, which might require security protection. Often, the software is developed to use external RACF security. If that is the case, then there are two choices, depending on your need:

- You can create your own RACF class or classes (more involved).

- You can use the FACILITY class.

If you use the FACILITY class, make sure your profiles are made unique, again by inserting your software product's abbreviation as part of the profile name.

FACILITY Class Profiles: A Word of Caution

Be careful about wide-open profiles defined in the FACILITY class. For example, if you have a profile STGADMIN.**, it could cover a wide range of storage management functions. Anyone with access to that profile would be eligible to use these powers if you did not have more specific profiles. The profile "**" in the FACILITY class would be even more risky and dangerous if not properly set up.

While these general profiles are risky in any class, they are especially so in the FACILITY class because of the very nature of this class. For more information, refer to chapter 11, "Security Administration: Beyond the Basics."

✓ How Secure Is *Your* Installation?

Enter the following RACF command:

```
RLIST FACILITY *
```

Do you see the "**" profile? If you do, what user IDs or RACF groups are in the access list of this profile? What is the universal access (UACC)?

Be very careful about the security risks associated with this profile.

7

The Benefits of the SEARCH Command

T he RACF SEARCH command is unlike any other. It does not update anything in the security database; it merely lists and reports on the information. So powerful are some of its search capabilities, however, that you can use the command to produce quick, simple reports, instead of programming them. In this sense, the command is a rudimentary reporting tool. (For a complete description of the SEARCH command, refer to IBM's *RACF Command Language Reference* manual.)

The best way to illustrate the usefulness of the SEARCH command is with examples. The examples in this chapter have been selected for their practical usefulness and to show the SEARCH command's wide-ranging applicability.

Note that, since even displaying security information by unauthorized users is an audit issue, you will need the SPECIAL or AUDITOR attribute to be able to get full results from the SEARCH command. More importantly, note that if you do not have these special powers, the SEARCH command will not say so—it will simply give partial results, which can be very confusing.

Creating RACF Commands

The example in this section illustrates a useful feature of the RACF SEARCH command, namely, the ability to *create* bulk RACF commands quickly, for later submission.

Suppose you want to remove WARNING mode from all profiles that have it specified. The following variation of the SEARCH command achieves this:

```
SEARCH FILTER(**) CLASS(DATASET) WARNING CLIST('ALTDSD ' ' NOWARNING GENERIC')
```

The results of this command will go to the data set called *userid*.EXEC.RACF.CLIST, where *userid* is your TSO user ID. The results will look like this:

```
ALTDSD 'ABC.TEST.**' NOWARNING GENERIC

ALTDSD 'DEF.*.DATA.**' NOWARNING GENERIC

. . . Etc.
```

You can now review these results to make sure you want to remove the WARNING mode from all these profiles. If appropriate, then simply run the commands:

```
EXEC 'userid.EXEC.RACF.CLIST'
```

Just by making good use of the SEARCH command, you have done away with an important audit issue.

Cleaning Up the RACF Database

The example in this section shows how you can do database cleanup work using the SEARCH command. Let's say you have an obsolete RACF class called OBSCLASS at your installation. You want to delete the class and all profiles defined to it.

To list all profiles in the OBSCLASS class, enter the following command:

```
SEARCH CLASS(OBSCLASS)
```

Now, using the CLIST keyword of the command described above, you can create bulk RACF commands to do the cleanup.

Listing Profiles, User IDs, and Groups

If you want to list all profiles protecting data sets for the VISA application, and these data sets have a high-level qualifier (HLQ) of VISA, you can enter the following command:

```
SEARCH CLASS(DATASET) MASK(VISA)
```

The results from this command might look like this:

```
VISA.PROD.** (G)

VISA.PR*.** (G)

VISA.TEST.** (G)

VISA.** (G)

. . . Etc.
```

You can list user IDs and RACF groups as well. The following command lists all user IDs at your installation that begin with ABC:

```
SEARCH CLASS(USER) MASK(ABC)
```

This next command will list all RACF groups that begin with PAY at your installation:

```
SEARCH CLASS(GROUP) MASK(PAY)
```

Revoking User IDs

One of the housekeeping activities of the security administration department is revoking user IDs not used for a certain time interval. Let's say you want to revoke user IDs not used in the past 100 days. The following command will give you the list of user IDs that fall into this category:

```
SEARCH CLASS(USER) AGE(100)
```

If, in addition, you want to generate bulk RACF commands to do the actual revoking, then extend the command to this:

```
SEARCH CLASS(USER) AGE(100) CLIST('ALTUSER ' ' REVOKE')  NOLIST
```

The sample output would look something like this:

```
ALTUSER SMITH03 REVOKE

ALTUSER CHAN02 REVOKE

ALTUSER SHARMA06 REVOKE

. . .  Etc.
```

Finally, you can run the commands by running this:

```
EXEC 'userid.EXEC.RACF.CLIST'
```

Caution: Be careful before you run these bulk RACF commands. Make sure you are not revoking seldom-used but still valid user IDs, such as those required for disaster recovery testing.

Finding Duplicate UIDs and GIDs

It is not recommended that you assign the same UID to more than one user, or the same GID to more than one group. Quite often, however, this can happen. The SEARCH command can help you find your duplicates.

The following command will show all users having the UID(0) specification (SUPERUSER privilege):

```
SEARCH CLASS(USER) UID(0)
```

Similarly, this command will show which groups are sharing this GID:

```
SEARCH CLASS(GROUP) GID(9876)
```

Searching a User's Access to Profiles

There are times when you want to know what profiles a user ID has access to in a particular class. The following command will list all profiles that user ID MARY08 has access to in the FACILITY class:

```
SEARCH USER(MARY08) CLASS(FACILITY)
```

Finding Discrete Profiles

In this last example, we will find all discrete—that is, non-generic—RACF profiles. These should not be confused with fully-qualified generic profiles, which look the same except for the (G) specification when you list them. (For more information about discrete profiles, see chapter 11, "Security Administration: Beyond the Basics.")

If you want to find all RACF discrete profiles at your installation with the intention of replacing them with generic ones, here is the SEARCH command:

```
SEARCH FILTER(**) CLASS(DATASET) NOGENERIC
```

Hopefully, you will not find any discrete profiles, but if you do and you want to replace them, you should first create their generic counterparts and then delete the discrete ones.

Summary

If you are not familiar with the SEARCH command, you should definitely spend some time learning more about it. It has many useful features. To learn more about these features, enter the following TSO command:

```
HELP SEARCH
```

You will be surprised at the number of different options it offers.

8

WARNING Mode and Its Implications

There are risks and costs to a program of action—
but they are far less than the long-range cost of comfortable inaction.
—John F. Kennedy

WARNING mode is a RACF feature that allows access to resources when other means (access lists, special privileges, universal access, and so on) would not have allowed access. Imagine. Security administrators spend a lot of time and effort setting up security, but profiles in WARNING mode override all that security!

What is worse, many security administrators do not even know the full implications of WARNING mode. They might not know that a profile in WARNING mode allows *full access to anyone, to access all resources protected by that profile*. This includes not only READ and UPDATE access but also the ability to delete the resources!

For this reason, WARNING mode, if used carelessly, can result in significant security exposures. It can nullify some of your security intentions and even compromise the integrity of your installation's data.

Of course, if a user does not qualify to get the access by other means, and gains the access solely because the profile is in WARNING mode, then that access is logged, and a warning message is issued to the user, telling him or her this is just temporary access. But even if the installation is mindful of these logs and is producing reports from them, there is no guarantee that these will be reviewed and followed up on in a timely manner.

In any case, the reporting happens after the fact, when the damage might have already been done.

The Proper Use of WARNING Mode

One may ask, if this feature carries with it so much risk, why is it there in the first place? The answer is, there is one very good use of WARNING mode. This involves putting profiles in WARNING mode on a *temporary* basis.

For example, if you want to implement security for a resource where there was none before, you might be rightly concerned about affecting users. Since until now the use of the resource was wide open, you cannot simply build profiles right away and hope it will not fail any legitimate user. Your plan of action should be to build security gradually by adding legitimate users to access lists.

The right approach is to build your profiles and put them in WARNING mode. This will allow users to access the resource like before, but if any access is granted by virtue of the profile being in WARNING mode, it will be logged. By reviewing these logs, you can monitor who is using the resource. If the user is justified, you can add him or her to the access lists of the profiles. Over time, you should see fewer users getting access by virtue of WARNING mode.

After a reasonable amount of time has elapsed, you will have identified all legitimate users. At this point, you should remove WARNING mode.

If used in this manner, WARNING mode can be a useful tool in a security administrator's toolkit.

The Incorrect Use of WARNING Mode

There is another, wrong reason why profiles are sometimes put in WARNING mode: an application might be having many security access failures, and the security administrators might be having a busy day. So, to "fix" the failures temporarily, they decide to put the applicable profile or profiles in WARNING mode. By allowing this "temporary" access, they have bypassed the proper solution, which is to analyze the failures and grant permissions as needed.

Sure, this will stop the failures from occurring. The problem with this method of solving access failures, however, is that WARNING mode will allow everyone full access to the resources. What is worse, since everyone is getting the accesses (rightful users as well as unauthorized ones), nobody will complain about access problems, and the WARNING mode is likely to go unnoticed. Over time, it will entrench itself and acquire permanent status. Eventually, nobody will dare to remove it, for fear of affecting authorized users.

If you do not remove WARNING mode after its purpose is over, legitimate users might start getting access without being in the access list. Then, it becomes difficult to simply remove WARNING mode, because now you have legitimate users who would be impacted if it were removed. The only way out of this dilemma would be to monitor the logs as mentioned above, as if the resource had no security.

Finding All Profiles in WARNING Mode

The easiest way to find all profiles in WARNING mode is to use the SEARCH command:

```
SEARCH FILTER(**) CLASS(DATASET) WARNING
```

You will need to do this for each active RACF class at your installation. For more information about the SEARCH command, refer to chapter 7, "The Benefits of the SEARCH Command."

Make Sure WARNING Mode Is Justified

You should periodically review all profiles in WARNING mode to verify their ongoing validity. Ideally, you should not find any such profiles. If you do, then you need to investigate.

This is where a lot of effort is required. The only profiles that are justified are those that are newly created, and where the access requirements are not clear, so the profiles have been put in WARNING mode to determine who needs access.

Remove WARNING Mode Where Inappropriate

When you have determined that a profile is incorrectly in WARNING mode, you will need to decide on appropriate additions to the access lists, using the logs described above. This will ensure that legitimate users will not lose the access they have been getting via WARNING mode. Once this is done, you can remove WARNING mode from the profiles.

Sometimes the difficult question is, how long do you monitor the logs before you stop looking for legitimate users? One month? Two months? How about users who could potentially be using these resources only once a year? To catch these users in logs, you would need to log and monitor for a year. How about the "occasional" legitimate users, who might need the resource at random, maybe not even once a year?

There is no clear answer. One approach to consider is to evaluate the importance of the resources covered by the profile. This will help determine the logging timeframe.

For less important resources, you might want to take a chance and remove WARNING mode right away. Those users who complain can be verified and added at that time.

Summary

Even though profiles in WARNING mode might cause security breaches, they do not stick out from the rest, so they might go unnoticed. Therefore, be very careful about putting profiles in WARNING mode in the first place. In this case, prevention is definitely better than the cure.

9

Understanding z/OS UNIX Security

U NIX comes in many flavors. In this chapter, we will discuss only z/OS UNIX, which is IBM's version of UNIX specifically meant for the z/OS operating system.

The original name for mainframe UNIX was "OpenEdition MVS," but that name is no longer used. It is now commonly referred to as z/OS UNIX System Services (USS), or simply, z/OS UNIX.

IBM added z/OS UNIX to the z/OS operating system after the popularity of UNIX grew. Today, z/OS UNIX plays a prominent role in some of the newer applications that are developed. These applications typically require interaction with distributed servers across the company's network.

Security features to protect z/OS UNIX resources were added to RACF over time, as the need arose. Initially, only the FACILITY class was used. (For more information, refer to chapter 6, "Understanding the FACILITY Class.") By convention, profiles in this class that are prefixed by BPX are meant to protect z/OS UNIX resources.

In subsequent versions, IBM introduced two new RACF classes to protect z/OS UNIX resources, UNIXMAP and UNIXPRIV. There is some overlap in protection mechanisms. This fact might cause some confusion for security practitioners, especially those not exposed to UNIX terminology.

UNIX has its own file system called HFS, the Hierarchical File System. In z/OS UNIX, the HFS data is stored as z/OS data sets. RACF can protect these data sets by normal means, that is, with RACF profiles in the DATASET class.

Security for the data residing inside these HFS data sets is also done in RACF, but this is where you need to understand new terms and concepts. The traditional role of RACF has been expanded to deal with a host of z/OS UNIX security requirements.

How z/OS UNIX Security Works

First, there are two basic RACF requirements before a person is able to use z/OS UNIX:

1. The person must have a RACF user ID, and that user ID must have an OMVS segment. (The segment is called the OMVS segment even though it would make more sense to call it the UNIX segment. The reason for this is historical. When UNIX was first introduced on MVS, the predecessor of z/OS, it was called OpenEdition MVS; hence, the segment name OMVS.)

2. The default group of the user ID must also have an OMVS segment.

UNIX data is stored in files. Its HFS file structure is completely different from the concept of data sets used in the z/OS environment. Rather, it is similar to the one used in Microsoft® Windows®-based PCs. Security information, consisting of flags, is kept within the file system, in File Security Packets (FSP). Within the FSP, there is the concept of the UID to represent the file owner, and the GID to represent the group owning the file. Access is given based on UID and GID information stored in the FSP.

On the RACF side, there is an OMVS segment in the RACF user ID profile (much like the CICS and TSO segments) that defines various UNIX attributes for the user, including the UID. There is also an OMVS segment in the default-group profile of the user ID that defines the GID.

When UNIX resources are accessed, security checking is done by calling RACF. RACF compares the UID and GID values of the UNIX resource to the UID and GID values assigned to the user ID in RACF. Therefore, the UID and GID values assigned or inherited by a user ID play an important part in z/OS UNIX.

Planning for z/OS UNIX Security

If your installation is going to deploy UNIX applications on the IBM mainframe environment, you will need to plan for and implement RACF security for z/OS UNIX.

Even if you don't plan to bring z/OS UNIX applications on board, you might still be required to implement some portions of RACF/UNIX security for other reasons. For example, to do file transfers between the mainframe and other platforms using FTP, you need z/OS UNIX and, therefore, RACF/UNIX security. TCP/IP and LDAP implementations are other examples.

It is important to have a plan that defines basic RACF security for a z/OS UNIX environment, so you will be positioned to exploit z/OS UNIX features more fully, if and when required. You will need to define policies and procedures to administer the z/OS UNIX environment, making decisions such as these:

- Who to allow to use z/OS UNIX

- What UIDs and GIDs to assign

- How to track assigned UID and GID values

- How to monitor and audit the UNIX environment

Without a plan, you might end up having undesirable results.

For example, use of FTP is quite common these days. Therefore, RACF administrators are asked to assign OMVS segments to users wanting to use

FTP. Without a plan, the RACF administrator might assign OMVS segments without much thought as to what UID and GID values to use. While this will work in the short term, it might have negative implications in the future, in which case some of the work will need to be re-done.

Unique UIDs and GIDs Recommended

Although UIDs and GIDs can be shared among users and groups, it is not recommended to do so. Since file protection in the HFS is done at the UID and GID level, sharing doesn't make sense because you lose accountability.

Only in exceptional cases might you want to share UIDs and GIDs. Ideally, each user should have a unique UID assigned, and each group a unique GID. The only exception is UID(0), which gives the user "superuser" powers. You might have more than one user requiring this.

The RACF class UNIXMAP keeps track of the use of UIDs and GIDs. It can be used to ensure that RACF users and groups have unique UIDs and GIDs. It is best to activate this class *before* you start assigning UIDs and GIDs at your installation.

If the UNIXMAP class was not active when you first started assigning UIDs and GIDs, then you will have to take some steps described in the *z/OS Security Server (RACF) System Administrator's Guide*. This involves running a REXX exec to "populate" the UNIXMAP class from the RACF database, and then activating the UNIXMAP class to keep track of future changes to UIDs and GIDs.

If the UNIXMAP class is active, you can query it to find out who is using a particular UID or GID, for example:

```
RLIST UNIXMAP G555 ALL
```

It is important to note that profiles in the UNIXMAP class are automatically created; you do not need to maintain the access list.

You might want to assign OMVS segments to all user IDs and to all groups, even though they might not require z/OS UNIX services. In that case, you can specify defaults, to be used by individuals who do not have any OMVS segments.

This is done via the FACILITY class profile BPX.DEFAULT.USER. It contains, in the APPLDATA field, the default RACF user ID and default RACF group ID, to be used for OMVS segment lookup purposes. You have to define the default user ID and the default group ID to RACF. Note that the defaults are only used in cases where no OMVS segment is present for the user. If an OMVS segment is found, then information from that segment, not from the default user ID's segment, is used.

The SUPERUSER Privilege

Perhaps the single most important issue in z/OS UNIX security is that of the SUPERUSER privilege. This is a very powerful privilege and can be compared to someone having the RACF attributes OPERATIONS, SPECIAL, and AUDITOR all at once.

There are three ways a user ID can acquire SUPERUSER powers:

- Having a UID value of zero, that is, UID(0) in the OMVS segment. This is the least desirable method but in practice is widely used at many installations.

- Having access via the BPX.SUPERUSER profile in the FACILITY class. This is an acceptable method, but it is not the one IBM recommends.

- Having access via the UNIXPRIV class. This is the method IBM recommends.

Note: The "conventional" RACF privileges and the UNIX privileges are mutually exclusive. A user ID having any of the RACF privileges OPERATIONS, SPECIAL, or AUDITOR does not get special powers in z/OS UNIX. Similarly, a user ID having SUPERUSER privilege has no special powers in the non-UNIX environment.

Even if SUPERUSER is warranted for a user ID, the best way to grant this capability is via the UNIXPRIV class, and not by means of assigning UID(0) in the user ID's OMVS segment.

If you have the UNIXMAP class active, you can see how many users have UID(0) assigned by entering this command:

```
RLIST UNIXMAP U0 ALL
```

If you do not have the UNIXMAP class active, you can enter the following command:

```
SEARCH CLASS(USER) UID(0)
```

Since SUPERUSER is such a powerful privilege, it is recommended that you do not give it to many users. Some users might need only a subset of the SUPERUSER powers. Giving them full powers is like giving a hotel guest the master key for the hotel, instead of just the key to one room. The RACF class called UNIXPRIV, described below, can be used to specify more granular portions of SUPERUSER powers.

Auditing z/OS UNIX

The following classes are available for auditing z/OS UNIX:

- DIRACC

- DIRSRCH

- FSOBJ

- FSSEC

- IPCOBJ

- PROCACT

- PROCESS

These classes do not need to be activated, nor can you create profiles in them.

Auditing does not happen automatically, however. In order to audit z/OS UNIX, you need to specify your audit options using one or both of the following commands for each of the above classes:

```
SETROPTS LOGOPTIONS
```

```
SETROPTS AUDIT
```

Implementing z/OS UNIX Controls

There are many things to consider when implementing z/OS UNIX security using RACF. For this reason, you might not want to implement all the controls right away. The best way is to implement the security gradually. This approach will allow you to make adjustments and do fine-tuning as you go along. Also, you are less likely to impact the UNIX users adversely.

z/OS UNIX concepts are quite different from what a security practitioner might have observed in the non-UNIX environment. For this reason, it is best to work with the z/OS UNIX administrators to implement these controls.

The bottom line for a security administrator is the same, however: most of the z/OS UNIX security implementation issues deal with creating RACF profiles in various classes and adding appropriate persons to the access lists. The important thing is to understand what each profile does, and its implications, as explained below.

FACILITY Class Considerations

In chapter 6, "Understanding the FACILITY Class," you saw that the prefix BPX is reserved for z/OS UNIX profiles. If a FACILITY class profile begins with BPX, then by convention it is a profile protecting a z/OS UNIX resource. Some of the BPX profiles available in earlier versions of RACF are now obsolete, or their functionality has been moved to the UNIXPRIV class.

Below is a list of FACILITY class profiles that apply to z/OS UNIX. In most cases, an access level of READ is sufficient to allow access:

- BPX.DEFAULT.USER—This profile defines, via the APPLDATA field, the default user ID and the default RACF group to be used for UID and GID purposes, when a user ID does not have an OMVS segment defined in his or her profile. It does not have anyone in the access list.

- BPX.SUPERUSER—User IDs having READ access to this profile can become "superusers" by issuing the SU UNIX command. This access should be restricted to only a few user IDs. The discussion on the UNIXPRIV class in the next section of this chapter explains how to grant only portions of the SUPERUSER privilege.

- BPX.DAEMON—A *daemon* is a UNIX term to denote an entity that is similar to a started task in z/OS. User IDs (daemons) having READ access to this profile can change their security identity to that of another user. A daemon might need to do this to perform a function on behalf of a user. (This is similar to the capability offered by the SURROGAT class for non-UNIX applications.) By assuming another user's identity, security checking is done under that user's privileges, and not the daemon's. The profile is there because not all daemons should be allowed to change their identities.

- BPX.**—This is the z/OS UNIX "back-stop" profile, sometimes also known as the "catch-all" profile. It is an important profile, since it is the one used if any of the more specific BPX profiles discussed above are not defined at your installation. Make sure it has universal access (UACC) of NONE, and that there is no one in the access list. (For more information about back-stop profiles, refer to chapter 11, "Security Administration: Beyond the Basics.")

  If this profile has UACC other than NONE, you might have serious security issues. Even if you do not have security exposures now, you will introduce them later in your environment if and when new z/OS UNIX controls are introduced via a BPX profile. If you do not already have this profile defined, then you might want to do so, but with proper care.

A word of caution before you define the bpx.** profile:

If you do not have all of the more specific profiles mentioned above defined, you might have legitimate users getting access via this back-stop profile. In that case, making universal access NONE right away might cause unintended failures. The best way is to grant universal access (UACC) of READ to this profile first and audit the profile. You can then monitor its use until such time as you are comfortable changing the universal access to NONE.

UNIXPRIV Class Considerations

The RACF UNIXPRIV class, as the name implies, is used solely for z/OS UNIX purposes. You will need to activate this class, if you have not already done so.

The UNIXPRIV class allows you to hand out only portions of the SUPERUSER powers to individuals. Since SUPERUSER is such a powerful authority, you might want to reserve that privilege for only a few users. For the rest, you should grant an appropriate subset of the SUPERUSER powers, as required.

If you already have a number of user IDs with the SUPERUSER privilege, it might be a good idea to consider removing that privilege from some of the users and granting them access to some of the UNIXPRIV class profiles instead.

For more information about how to use profiles in the UNIXPRIV class, refer to the IBM manual *z/OS Security Server RACF Security Administration Guide*, specifically the section "Using UNIXPRIV class profiles to manage z/OS UNIX privileges."

Other z/OS UNIX Considerations

So far, we have discussed z/OS UNIX security in the RACF classes FACILITY, UNIXMAP, and UNIXPRIV. These cover almost all the z/OS UNIX security implementation issues.

However, you also need to consider the following from a "conventional" RACF point of view:

- You need to define STARTED class profiles for the started tasks OMVS (OMVS.*) and BPXOINIT (BPXOINIT.*).

- You need to use the PROGRAM class if you wish to control daemon authority via this class. If you do this, you might find that there are several libraries that you will need to identify and control via the PROGRAM class also (for example, SYS1.LINKLIB).

- You need to provide RACF protection for the UNIX HFS data sets. These data sets are normal z/OS data sets as far as RACF protection goes. If your UNIX HFS datasets have the prefix HFS.OMVS, then create a profile HFS.OMVS.**. You might want to give universal access of READ to this profile, and give ALTER access to the started task OMVSKERN.

To summarize, even some long-time RACF security practitioners find it difficult to understand z/OS UNIX security. This is simply because it is relatively new, and because some of the concepts are different from the traditional z/OS platform. However, z/OS UNIX is growing in popularity, and today many applications interface with this newer technology. The most important point to keep in mind is the risk associated with too many users having the SUPERUSER privilege.

✓ How Secure Is *Your* Installation?

Count the number of user IDs at your installation that have UID(0) in their OMVS segment. Do all these user IDs need the full capabilities of the SUPERUSER privilege? If not, then you need to start a project to make greater use of the UNIXPRIV class and grant only portions of the SUPERUSER powers.

10

The Benefits of RACF Commands in Batch Mode

The batch processing of RACF commands, when appropriate, can increase your productivity manifold. Not only is this method faster, it is also less error-prone. Running RACF commands in batch mode, however, requires a good understanding of JCL.

The best way to learn batch mode is by practicing. Practice using batch mode whenever an opportunity arises. This way you will learn, and at the same time be more productive. Even if opportunities do not arise, find some trivial reason to practice in your spare time. Remember, however, that in the beginning, you should only experiment with "list" type RACF commands, so you do not affect production work.

In this chapter, you will discover some of the instances where batch mode is very useful.

Capturing the Results of RACF Commands

In most cases, it is enough to enter RACF commands in ISPF, using option 6, and get your results on the screen. There are times, however, when you want to do more than simply view the output on your screen: you want to save the output in a data set for review, for reporting, or for audit purposes.

In these cases, using batch mode will help. When you run RACF commands in batch mode, you have the ability to save the results of your commands in a data set for future reference.

The ISPF RACF commands do not allow you to do this. One solution is to use the "cut and paste" method to copy the results from the screen to a data set. However, your RACF command might generate a lot of output. So this method is not only cumbersome; it can also be time-consuming and error-prone.

Let's say we want to list all user IDs in the RACF database and save the results for future reference. The RACF command for this is LISTUSER *. The following is sample JCL to do this. You might have to change it to conform to your installation's JCL standards:

```
//MYJOB001  JOB 'YOUR NAME',MSGCLASS=X,CLASS=A,NOTIFY=&SYSUID

//STEP01 EXEC PGM=IKJEFT01,REGION=1M

//SYSTSPRT DD DSN=USERID.RACF.ALL.USERS,DISP=(NEW,CATLG),

//  SPACE=(CYL,(10,10))

//SYSTSIN  DD *

LISTUSER *

/*
```

The RACF commands are specified after the SYSTSIN DD statement. In this case, the command we want to execute in batch mode is LISTUSER *.

When you run this JCL, the results of the RACF command will go to the data set specified in the SYSTSPRT DD statement. In this case, the name is

USERID.RACF.ALL.USERS. You have now accomplished your goal of listing all user IDs in this data set, using batch mode.

Automating a Process

Suppose you want to use the above method to create a list of all RACF users once a week. One option is to remember to run the JCL every week, but this obviously has its drawbacks.

Using batch mode and your scheduling software, it is possible to automate this process. Simply specify to the scheduling software that you want to run the JCL every week. By automating the task, you have not only removed the possibility of forgetting it; there is also one less activity for you to do, so you can concentrate on other important tasks.

Performing an Action Repeatedly

Suppose you want to list the RACF global options periodically and keep your results in a partitioned data set (PDS). Using ISPF, you can view the global options on your screen, but you will not be able to save the results for later review. Batch mode provides the answer.

The RACF command to list RACF global options is SETROPTS LIST.

In this sample JCL, your output will go to the PDS YOUR.DATASET.NAME, in member name LIST1:

```
//RACFJOB1  JOB 'YOUR NAME',MSGCLASS=X,CLASS=A,NOTIFY=&SYSUID
//STEP01 EXEC PGM=IKJEFT01,REGION=1M
//SYSTSPRT DD DSN=YOUR.DATASET.NAME(LIST1),DISP=SHR
//SYSTSIN  DD *
SETROPTS LIST
/*
```

Every time you run this JCL, all you have to do is change the member name, for example, LIST2, LIST3, and so on.

Entering Groups of RACF Commands

Let's say you have a task that requires more than one RACF command, and you need to save the result whenever you perform this task. By using batch mode, you remove the need to remember a series of RACF commands.

A simple example of this would be to build a process to always list a user ID before deleting it and to save the result for future reference. Not only do you have the user ID's details if you ever need to restore the user ID, but you also know what user ID you deleted, and when. This is standard practice at many installations.

In this case, the commands you want to enter repeatedly for all deletions of user IDs are as follows (you will need to change the user ID every time):

```
LISTUSER LINDA22
```

```
DELUSER LINDA22
```

Here is the sample JCL you need to do this in batch mode:

```
//RACFJOB1  JOB 1,'YOUR NAME',MSGCLASS=X,CLASS=A,NOTIFY=&SYSUID

//STEP01 EXEC PGM=IKJEFT01,REGION=1M

//SYSTSPRT DD DSN=YOUR.DATASET.NAME(LINDA22),DISP=SHR

//SYSTSIN  DD *

LISTUSER LINDA22

DELUSER LINDA22

/*
```

As you can see, you can have as many RACF commands as you wish, all of them following the JCL statement //SYSTSIN DD *.

When Batch Mode Is the Only Method

Lastly, there are times when you must use batch mode to accomplish a task because it cannot be done using ISPF commands. One example of this is when you want to run the RACF database unload utility program. For more information about this, refer to chapter 26, "The RACF Unload Database."

Summary

Because of all the advantages of using batch mode, you should practice using this method whenever it is appropriate. Batch mode is particularly useful when doing RACF project work, but even in your daily administration work, there are benefits.

11

Security Administration: Beyond the Basics

We will bankrupt ourselves in the vain search for absolute security.
—Dwight D. Eisenhower

T here is no such thing as absolute, total security.

Corporations strive for enough security to meet their business needs. Anything beyond that would constitute a wasteful expense. Of course, different companies have different security needs. For example, companies developing new software might not need too much security—they would want to give as much freedom to their software developers as possible, and not encumber them with security-related restrictions. On the other hand, a bank protecting its credit card systems and client accounts would have to have a full-blown security set-up, complete with a security department protecting the corporate data.

All large companies—and many small ones, too—have a security administration group whose job it is to guard the company's information assets and maintain the rules that allow access to staff members and other users. Access is often granted on a need-to-know basis; that is, staff members should only have access to the information required for their jobs.

In this sense, the security administrators are the guardians of all information. Their job is to deal with the issue "who can do what" on the mainframe, in security terms. Grouping users and data simplifies their administration functions.

Security administration has evolved over the years into a specialized discipline. It is not to be taken lightly, and any organization that neglects appropriate staffing for this important function does so at its peril.

Security administration is a tactical function, as opposed to a strategic one. (The role of the security officer, on the other hand, is a strategic one.) It is a daily grind, where the team members are called upon to provide or remove security because of one of several reasons:

- New staff coming in

- Staff members leaving, retiring, or being let go

- Staff members transferring to different departments, and thus having different security requirements

- New applications coming in or old ones being phased out

- Staff members being promoted to different roles

Doing It Right the First Time

It is a mistake to think that anyone can do the job of a security administrator. Some organizations relegate this function to the Help Desk, which is a big mistake. Doing so for simple reasons such as password resets or "computer not working" type of issues is fine, but mainframe security administration is much more than that. If not done properly, it will end up costing the corporation more in the long run.

Quick-fix security administration, while solving the immediate issue at hand, causes more work at a future date. This extra work will manifest itself as a large project to clean up and "de-clutter" the security definitions in the security database. Consultants might have to be brought in to deal with this one-time project, further raising the costs.

A lapse in proper security actions might also result in too much access being granted, or worse, wrong access being granted. Both scenarios are likely to raise audit issues, at which time fixing the access permissions will end up costing more.

In a sense, security administration is an art. The more experienced the person is, the better the job he or she can do. While this is generally true in any job function, it is especially so in the case of security administration.

For example, if a customer requests access to a certain data set, the fastest way would be to add the person's user ID to the access list of the appropriate profile.

While this might be the fastest way, it may not be the best. There might be ten other people in the same group, who will make the same request in the days to come. Being able to foresee that need, and providing access to the whole group at the group level, as opposed to at the individual level, will save considerable time and effort in the future.

Recognizing this, however, requires both experience and foresight. Doing it right the first time has the obvious benefit of saving a lot of time later on. In this example, the other individuals would not have to make the same request, because they would already have the necessary access.

If the security administration team is not adequately staffed, administrators might even grant more access than is required. For example, suppose a request is made to grant READ access to user ID MIKE27 to the specific data set PAYROLL.JAN.REPORTS. Overworked administrators, in their haste, might not bother to create a separate profile for this, and might simply add the user ID to the existing profile PAYROLL.**. This, of course, will not raise any immediate issues because user ID MIKE27 has got what he wants, plus a lot more access!

This is like a hotel clerk giving a guest the master key for the entire hotel, instead of just the key to the guest's room.

It is in the best interest of the companies to hire competent security administrators, and not to overwork them to the point where they make these mistakes.

The role of the security administrator is an important job function. First, the administrator needs to know at least the working of the organization's security product, such as RACF. This is a good start, but it is by no means enough. He or she must also have an understanding of a number of security concepts and issues. These skills are only acquired over time.

In a typical month, a security administrator has to face a myriad of challenges. There is constant learning, and to become an expert takes several years.

Being Inquisitive

Security administrators should adopt an inquisitive mind-set. That way, they will constantly be increasing their knowledge. Just as a good detective asks questions about the seemingly minor details of a case, so it is with a smart security practitioner.

Two examples will suffice.

Being Inquisitive, Example 1

In April 2013, a beginner to RACF notices that the "last access date" displayed for the user ID GUPTA10 is November 2012. The installation has a policy of automatically revoking user IDs not used in the last 90 days. Based on this fact, the user ID should have been automatically revoked. However, when you list this user ID, it is not revoked; it does not show the REVOKE attribute assigned.

What is going on?

If the beginner persisted in finding the answer, he or she would learn that the user ID is indeed revoked, but RACF will not display it as revoked—at least, not until the user next tries to log onto the system. When the user tries to log on the next time, the system will display a message saying that the user ID is revoked, and the logon process will fail. The user ID will need to be resumed by a security administrator before the user can successfully log on.

If RACF did not behave this way, it would need to go through the entire RACF database every day, to figure out which user IDs are inactive more than 90 days, by comparing the current date with the last-used date of every user ID. For a RACF database with several thousand user IDs, this would take considerable time and system overhead every day.

Instead, it is much simpler (and faster) for RACF to figure out who is revoked at logon time, by comparing the current date to the last-used date for the user ID. That is the time the user ID is marked as inactive by assigning it the REVOKE attribute.

Such are the intricacies of RACF.

Being Inquisitive, Example 2

As another example of being inquisitive, suppose you notice that RACF allows *any* user to change their password interval using the PASSWORD command. (The password interval specifies the maximum number of elapsed days allowed between password changes. RACF forces you to change your password after the specified password interval has elapsed.)

If anyone is allowed to change their password interval, does this not contravene the installation's password interval policy? Why allow a user to bypass installation-wide standards?

Upon further reading and research, you find that it is true that a user can change the password interval, without any special privilege or authority. However, the user can only *decrease* the interval value, not *increase* it. Essentially, RACF is saying that if you want to reduce the password change interval, you are making yourself more secure than the installation-wide standards. However, if you want to *increase* the password change interval, you cannot, since that would be contravening installation-wide standards. To do that would require special powers.

Understanding RACF User Profile Segments

RACF user profiles can have *segments* attached to them. Segments are RACF profile extensions. They provide additional functions and capabilities to the holder of the profile. These capabilities are for access to major system functions such as TSO, CICS, and z/OS UNIX. There is a separate segment for each major function.

Not all user profiles need to have segments, and some can have more than one segment. For example, if a person needs to use both CICS and TSO, then that person's user profile will show two segments, one for CICS and one for TSO:

| BASIC Profile | TSO Segment | CICS Segment |

A CICS segment attached to a user profile allows that person to sign onto CICS. If this segment is missing, the person cannot use CICS. Similarly, if a person wants to use TSO, then their user profile must have a TSO segment. This makes it easy to control the use of CICS, TSO, z/OS UNIX, and so on.

To see whether user ID CHAN04 is allowed to use CICS, you can list the user ID with the following specification:

```
LISTUSER CHAN04 CICS
```

If the CICS segment is displayed, then CHAN04 is allowed to use CICS.

You can enter the HELP ADDUSER command in TSO to see all user profile segments available for use.

Quiz 11.1 explains a RACF user profile segment that is used for storage management purposes.

Quiz 11.1

1. What is the DFP segment in user profiles and in group profiles?

   Answer: The DFP segment has more to do with storage management than security. IBM is simply utilizing RACF segment information to facilitate storage management controls. The DFP segment specifies how the user ID's new data sets are to be managed for storage purposes.

   The DFP segment is optional. If one is specified in a user profile, it overrides the DFP segment information contained in the user's default-group profile, if it is specified there. Here is a sample DFP segment:

   DFP INFORMATION:
   MGMTCLAS= ARCHBAT
   STORCLAS= TSODISK
   DATACLAS= DCLASST
   DATAAPPL= APPL1

   Further, if a DFP class is not specified in the user profile's DFP segment, but is specified in the user's default-group profile, then that DFP class is used. If it is specified in the default-group profile and in the user profile, then the one in the user profile takes precedence.

   Quite often, users having the same default-group have similar storage management requirements. In that case, it helps to specify DFP class information at the group ID level, and not at the user ID level, to simplify RACF administration.

What Is a RACF Discrete Profile?

What is a RACF discrete profile, and why are discrete profiles still there?

Many years ago, when RACF was first introduced, data sets on disk were protected by means of *discrete* profiles. The protection of data depended on the disk volume on which the data sets resided. You had to specify the volume serial number of the disk in the command.

This method of protection has obvious drawbacks, especially now, when it does not matter which disk volume the data resides on. Also, automated storage management programs such as DFHSM are likely to move data from one disk to another, based on storage management criteria.

Later, IBM introduced generic profiles in RACF. It did not matter anymore where the data set resided. Most installations use these generic profiles.

Despite the drawbacks of discrete profiles, some installations still may have them. These might be leftovers from the distant past. In some cases, they might have been created more recently, by mistake.

If you are creating a data set profile without any "wildcard" characters, specify the keyword GENERIC at the end of the command, like this:

```
ADDSD 'VISA.PROD.DATA SET' OWNER(ABC) GENERIC
```

Otherwise, RACF will create a discrete profile!

For information about how to search for all discrete profiles at your installation, refer to chapter 7, "The Benefits of the SEARCH Command."

What Are Undefined RACF User IDs?

Undefined user IDs are those that have entered the system, but for which there is no RACF user profile.

If a batch job that runs on your system has no user ID to work with (usually via a remote node using Remote Job Entry, RJE, but possibly internally), the job will acquire a "default" user ID, as specified in your RACF global options.

It is up to the installation whether to allow undefined user IDs to run on your system. To see what is specified at your installation, enter the following command:

```
SETROPTS LIST
```

Suppose you see this specification:

```
JES (UNDEFINEDUSER (DFTUSR))
```

In this case, the "undefined default" user ID for your installation is DFTUSR.

It is quite common to allow such undefined user IDs to enter the system, to support RJE processing. Ideally, this undefined user ID will have been granted minimal access, so RJE jobs coming into your system will not be able to do much on your system.

The next section contains more information about "undefined" RACF user IDs.

Universal Access (UACC) Considerations

If you want everyone to have, say, READ access to a profile, there are two ways to do it:

1. You can specify the profile's universal access as READ.

2. You can specify the general entry ID(*) READ in the access list of the profile.

While both of these methods will provide READ access, there is a subtle difference. The universal access applies to "undefined" RACF user IDs mentioned in the previous section, as well as to "defined" user IDs, that is, those that have RACF user profiles. The general entry in the access list applies only to "defined" RACF user IDs.

It is therefore a good security practice to always have a universal access of NONE specified for all your profiles (DATASET and RESOURCE), and to specify general access via the access list, if applicable. If you do not do this, you might have a security exposure.

The only exceptions would be for resources that pose little risk if accessed by remote batch jobs without a defined RACF user ID, or in cases where you know there is a need for such remote batch jobs to access the data.

If you have universal access other than NONE specified in a profile, and you want to remove this security exposure, first make sure you do not have remote batch requirements for undefined RACF user IDs needing access. Then, do the following:

1. Change the profile to have UACC(NONE).

2. Add general access, ID(*), to the same profile.

The Restricted Attribute

Usually, a RACF attribute grants more powers to a user ID. The RESTRICTED attribute, however, *prevents* a user ID from having access that he or she would otherwise have had. A user ID having this attribute will not get access specified in any of these three places:

- Universal access (UACC)

- General access specified by ID(*) in the access list

- The Global Access Checking (GAC) table

The only access the user ID will get is where it is explicitly mentioned by user ID in the access list, or if it belongs to a RACF group that is specified in the access list.

The RESTRICTED attribute can be viewed as the converse of the OPERATIONS privilege, which grants access unless specifically prevented. The RESTRICTED attribute is RACF's way of preventing a user from getting the three types of general accesses mentioned above.

Disaster Recovery Considerations

Disaster recovery is sometimes referred to as contingency planning. It involves dealing with the unlikely scenario whereby your physical computer site is not able to operate for any reason, and you have to go to a pre-arranged backup site for processing all your business-critical computing. If that were to happen, you would first have to restore your production operating environment as fast as possible.

The security department is often involved in disaster recovery planning. In addition, the security department is often called upon to provide support during an actual disaster recovery test.

In security terms, you need to create a powerful user ID with full privileges, including OPERATIONS, SPECIAL and AUDITOR, to be used only during disaster testing. This user ID should be kept in REVOKED state during normal processing. During disaster testing, you can either activate the user ID from the Master Console or do this before you take your disk backups for testing.

What Are RACF "Grouping Classes"?

Some RACF resource classes allow you to group profiles having similar access requirements. CICS classes are the best example of this.

In the case of CICS, you would want to group similar transactions if they have similar access requirements. Now, this is easy if the transaction names themselves allow you to do the grouping. For example, if there are three payroll transactions, PAY1, PAY2, and PAY3, it is easy to group them by creating a profile PAY* that covers all three of them.

But what if you have payroll transactions called HOURPAY, PAY1, SALARY, and WAGES, and they all have similar access requirements? The above method of simply using "wildcarding" does not work.

This is where grouping classes come in. Using grouping classes, you can create a profile called PAYROLL and add all four transactions mentioned above to that profile. Now, all four transactions can be treated equally for access purposes.

Grouping classes do not make sense for all RACF classes. For example, the DATASET class does not allow such grouping.

What Is RACF "Undercutting"?

Undercutting is the RACF term used when someone who previously had some access loses it inadvertently as a result of an oversight by a security administrator. This happens when a new profile is defined without proper care being taken not to undercut anyone's access.

Consider a scenario in which user ID MARY123, together with many other users, has READ access to PAYROLL.**, which covers all data sets beginning with the word PAYROLL.

A request comes in to tighten payroll data, and to create a new profile, PAYROLL.PROD.DATA, where the batch ID BATCH01 needs to have access. In response, you create the new profile with only the batch ID BATCH01 in the access list. All of a sudden, MARY123, who previously had access to PAYROLL. PROD.DATA, loses it. This is undercutting.

This happens because of the way RACF does its access checking. It looks for and uses the most specific profile that matches an access request. In this case, as soon as the profile PAYROLL.PROD.DATA was created, it was used for access checking, and not the more general profile, PAYROLL.**.

To avoid undercutting users from any access they already have, you have to be careful before you create more specific profiles. You need to look at all profiles that are more general than the one you are creating and carry forward the accesses to the new profile. (The exception, of course, is when you are specifically told that the new profile is created by design, to lock out the more general profile users.)

Undercutting can happen for general resource classes, also.

What Is a RACF "Back-Stop" Profile?

The back-stop profile is sometimes also called the *catch-all* profile. This profile is used when RACF finds no other match during access checking in the given class of resource. It is the most general profile in a particular group of profiles.

Back-stop profiles play an important role. Without them, many of the resources that you have not thought of will not have proper protection. By creating a back-stop profile, you ensure that current, and any future, resources will be covered by the back-stop profile.

The importance of the back-stop profile, and its relevance to security, is best described with an example. Let's say you have these profiles for z/OS UNIX in the FACILITY class:

- BPX.DEFAULT.USER

- BPX.SUPERUSER

- BPX.**

Now let's say RACF is checking for the resource BPX.DAEMON in the FACILITY class. Since there is no specific profile for this resource, the profile BPX.** is used for access checking. There could be many more resources also covered by this profile.

In this case, BPX.** is called the back-stop profile. It "back-stops" everything that does not have a more specific BPX.*something* defined.

The risk is that if a back-stop profile gives out wide-ranging access such as UACC(READ), you might have a security exposure because of the large number of potential resources that could fall under the profile. It is, therefore, a good security practice to keep to a minimum the universal access granted by a back-stop profile. Further, the access list for these profiles should be scrutinized to make sure you are not unintentionally giving out wide-ranging powers.

Why User IDs Must Not Be Shared

Some companies allow sharing of user IDs. This practice can lead to security concerns, as there is no accountability for the use of a shared user ID.

When a security violation occurs under the user ID, there is no sure way to find out who did it. On top of that, when a user ID is shared by multiple users, it implies that the password is also shared. This leads to passwords being written down, which are then at a higher risk of being compromised.

Granting Temporary Access to Resources

There are times when you want to grant access to a resource, but only for a limited time. For example, during the course of an audit, you might want to grant some access to an auditor. Another case is where someone is filling in for another person's job function temporarily.

One way to accomplish this is by making a note to revoke the access after the need is gone. This method is manual, however, and can cause security breaches if the access is not taken away in time.

A neater way is to make use of the fact that you can connect a user ID to a group, and make that connection effective on a certain date, or until a given date. Using this method, you can simply create a new group and grant that group the required access. Then, you connect the user ID to the group.

For example, to grant the user ID JONES access to start on a certain date, use this command:

```
CONNECT JONES GROUP(GRPTMP) RESUME(date)
```

To grant JONES access only until a future date, use this command:

```
CONNECT JONES GROUP(GRPTMP) REVOKE(date)
```

Even though the group will have permanent access, the user ID will be connected only temporarily to the group. Therefore, the user's access will be only temporary.

Creating "Fully-Qualified" Generic Profiles

Many z/OS operating system data sets are considered critical. Examples of these are SYS1.LINKLIB, SYS1.PROCLIB, and SYS1.LPALIB. All installations also have other business-specific data sets that are deemed critical to the running of their business. Examples of these are the payroll master file, customer lists, and data sets containing credit card information.

All these critical data sets should be protected by "fully-qualified" generic profiles. They should not be protected by more generic profiles.

For example, the data set SYS1.LINKLIB should be protected by the fully-qualified generic profile SYS1.LINKLIB, not by SYS1.** or by SYS1.LINK*. The reason for this is that if these critical data sets were protected by a profile that also protected other data sets, it is likely that the access list of this profile is a watered-down version of what is appropriate for these important data sets.

Make sure you have a fully-qualified generic profile for each important data set. That way, you can specify in the access list only the users needing access to them. Another benefit is that you will be able to specify more secure auditing criteria for this profile, which is not possible when you have a more general profile, as it would have created many unwanted audit records.

Note that, when defining a fully-qualified generic profile, you need to add GENERIC at the end of the command, to make sure you are creating a generic profile, like this:

```
ADDSD 'SYS1.PARMLIB' UACC(NONE) OWNER(ADMIN) GENERIC
```

Specifying Strong Passwords

RACF allows several password options. To list the options in effect at your installation, enter the following command:

```
SETROPTS LIST
```

Here are guidelines for enforcing strong passwords:

1. The minimum password length should be more than six characters.

2. There should be at least one numeric.

3. Passwords should be changed every 30 days for general users, and more often for users holding special privileges, such as operators and system programmers.

4. The previous 12 passwords should not be allowed to be reused.

RACF Global Options

RACF global options are displayed and modified using the SETROPTS command. You need the SPECIAL privilege to list or modify RACF global options. Even to display the settings, you need the AUDITOR attribute. (RACF global options are described throughout the book in appropriate chapters.)

———————————

Quiz 11.2 helps explain and clarify some of the concepts that a novice RACF person might need to know to perform daily security administration duties.

Quiz 11.2

1. If your installation has a data set profile, PAYROLL.**, how do you know which data sets it is actually protecting?

Answer: The following RACF command will answer this question:

LISTDSD DA('PAYROLL.**') DSN

It will list all the data sets that are being protected by the profile. If you find it is not protecting any data set, that means the profile is an obsolete one—it can be deleted.

This command will also be able to answer another question: do you need more granular profiles for sensitive data sets?

For example, you might find that this profile covers several sensitive data sets, all of them starting with PAYROLL.PROD. You might want to create a profile for just these sensitive data sets. In this case, create a profile, PAYROLL.PROD.**, with its own access list, which can be more restrictive than the general profile. This new profile will, of course, override the profile PAYROLL.**, since during access checking RACF always uses the most specific profile it finds.

Note that this command applies only to data set profiles, and not to any other general resource profiles.

2. Conversely, if you have a data set, SYS1.PROCLIB, how do you know which RACF profile protects it?

   Answer: Enter the following RACF command:

   LISTDSD DA('SYS1.LINKLIB') GENERIC

   It will show you the profile that is the closest match for the data set, and hence protects it. This command applies only to data sets, not general resources.

3. When you grant access via the PERMIT command, what is the difference between CONTROL access and UPDATE access?

   Answer: For data set profiles, the difference is very minor, but it is important when it comes to VSAM data sets. UPDATE access will allow most updates to VSAM data sets, but not all. To allow all updates, you need to specify CONTROL access. For non-VSAM data sets, UPDATE access is the same as CONTROL access.

   When creating a new data set profile, you don't know whether the profile covers VSAM data sets (or will cover them in the future). Therefore, you should always specify CONTROL access even when UPDATE access was requested.

   Do not automatically do this for *resource* profiles, however. For these, it can make a big difference: depending on the resource class, CONTROL can have an entirely different meaning than UPDATE.

4. What does the user ID IBMUSER do?

   Answer: The user ID IBMUSER is supplied with RACF. It has special privileges and is used to build your RACF environment, including creating other user IDs with special privileges so the installation can function.

Once you have built other user IDs with special privileges, you do not need IBMUSER. It should not be used for daily security administration, as it is not tied to an individual, and therefore you would lose accountability.

IBMUSER comes with a default password, documented in IBM manuals. So, the first thing you should do is change this default password to prevent its misuse. IBMUSER cannot be deleted. After you have built your RACF system, you should revoke it.

5. What is the EXECUTE level access in RACF?

   Answer: The EXECUTE level access for data set profiles has meaning when the data sets being protected by the profile are PDS libraries containing programs. It allows the user ID to execute the program from the library, but not to copy it.

   It is more restrictive than READ access, as READ also allows copying the programs from the library. The EXECUTE level access is useful in cases where you do not want to give the users the ability to copy programs, just to run them.

6. How do access levels in resource profiles differ from those in data set profiles?

   Answer: There is significant difference between the two.

   For data set profiles, the interpretation of access levels is fixed; there is only one meaning in all cases.

   For resource profiles, the interpretation varies from class to class. The only way to find out the meaning for sure is to look up the IBM manuals for IBM-provided resource classes. If the resource class is a non-IBM one, then you need to look up the non-IBM documentation for that class.

7. The SETROPTS LIST command at your installation may contain the following information:

ADDCREATOR IS NOT IN EFFECT

What does this mean?

Answer: The reason for the existence of the ADDCREATOR keyword is historical. When RACF was introduced, it worked as follows: if a user created a RACF profile, the user ("creator," in this case) was automatically added to the access list, with ALTER (full) access. One reason RACF was designed this way was that if a person had the ability to create a profile, that person must also own it, and therefore allowing full access was not a problem.

Later, IBM must have realized that this reasoning was not acceptable in all cases. The security practitioner creating a profile should not necessarily have access to the underlying data. His or her job is simply to administer security.

Some installations even adopted the practice of immediately removing the creator's user ID from the access list after a profile was created, leading to extra work, with no guarantee that this practice would always be followed.

IBM cannot simply reverse RACF functionality once it is introduced. So, it solved the dilemma by providing the option to not add the "creator" to the access list of the profile. Hence, two more keywords were introduced to the RACF command SETROPTS: ADDCREATOR and NOADDCREATOR.

Your installation will be more secure if you use the NOADDCREATOR option. Your SETROPTS LIST command should therefore show the following:

ADDCREATOR IS NOT IN EFFECT

Summary

In this chapter, we discussed some of the security administration issues that go beyond what a beginner to RACF might know. The topics were selected to broaden a beginner's perspective, and they should be viewed as such. No attempt has been made to exhaust the list of all possible scenarios.

✓ How Secure Is *Your* Installation?

Enter the RACF command SETROPTS LIST and see whether you find the following:

ADDCREATOR IS IN EFFECT

If you do, then you can have a security exposure.

Also, look at your FACILITY class profiles. Do you have back-stop profiles for each category, such as BPX and STGADMIN? If you don't, then you need to define them, but only after care has been taken to make sure current users will not fail.

The FACILITY class is not the only class that requires back-stop profiles.

PART TWO

SECURING THE z/OS OPERATING SYSTEM

Better be despised for too anxious apprehensions,
than ruined by too confident security.
—Edmund Burke

For security professionals, protecting the corporation's business data is an important task. This subject was covered in the first part of this book. In part 2, we will look at another area of mainframe security: protecting the z/OS operating system.

While business assets must be guarded to avoid direct losses to a company, the operating system must be guarded to avoid indirect losses. Potential issues include the entire system being unavailable, widespread system disruptions, loss of business data integrity, and even outright fraud.

The topic of protecting the operating system is a vast one. There is much vulnerability, and the sheer complexity of the operating system makes addressing all areas a daunting task.

The operating system has many components, and some of them are optional. Therefore, no two mainframe installations are likely to be identical. One company might have DB2, for example, and another might have IMS. Yet another might have DB2 *and* IMS.

When dealing with operating system security, it is best to cover the common ground, that is, issues common to all installations. These issues are presented in the following chapters. For each vulnerable area, the security exposure is described, followed by the risk factors, and finally appropriate ways to mitigate the risk.

12

APF-Authorized Libraries

APF stands for "Authorized Program Facility." APF-authorized libraries contain APF-authorized programs—these programs can bypass normal mainframe security.

Such powerful programs (and the libraries that house them) are needed because many operating system functions need to bypass normal mainframe security in order to perform their functions. Other optional operating system components such as DB2, IMS, and CICS also require some of their programs to bypass normal security.

It is safe to say that APF-authorized libraries belong to, or are extensions of, the z/OS operating system. The task of a security practitioner is therefore to guard these libraries from unintended program additions, deletions, or modifications.

What Is the Risk?

One of the biggest threats of a security breach at a mainframe installation may very well come from misuse of an APF-authorized library. Hackers wanting to harm your computer installation will look first and foremost for an unguarded APF-authorized library. If they manage to find one of these libraries, they can add their own program into it. Via this rogue program, they will be able to do considerable harm to the company's business assets by bypassing not just RACF security but also the built-in mainframe security.

Despite these risks, the proper protection of APF-authorized libraries is often overlooked. System programmers using these libraries for legitimate reasons are quite content as long as they have access to them. On the other hand, security practitioners often do not understand the full implication of this potential security exposure. Many of them have not even heard of APF-authorized libraries.

Finding APF-Authorized Libraries

To see whether APF-authorized libraries are adequately protected, the first task of a security practitioner is to find all of these libraries.

APF-authorized libraries are listed in various members of SYS1.PARMLIB and other parameter libraries you might have designated at your installation. It is difficult to manually search all these places and come up with a complete list. And each installation has its own, unique list.

A better method is to use the Data Security Monitor (DSMON) Selected Data Sets report. In order not to miss any LPA APF-authorized libraries, you should define your LPA, MLPA, and FLPA libraries in the applicable IEAAPF*xx* or PROG*xx* members of SYS1.PARMLIB also.

Here is a partial sample report:

S E L E C T E D	D A T A	S E T S	R E P O R T		
DATA SET NAME	VOLUME	SELECTION	RACF	RACF	UACC
	SERIAL	CRITERION	INDICATED	PROTECTED	
------------	-------	---------	---------	---------	------
SYS1.MQ.LOADLIB	SYSVOL	APF	N	NF	READ
DB2.LOADLIB	SYSVOL	APF	N	Y	UPDATE
SYS3.CICSLOAD	VOL123	APF	N	Y	READ
. . .					
SYS3.VEND.AUTH	VOL123	APF	N	Y	READ

For more information about DSMON, refer to chapter 3, "The Data Security Monitor (DSMON)."

How Do You Mitigate This Risk?

In the DSMON Selected Data Sets report, you might find you have dozens of APF-authorized libraries. You need to do several things, listed below. (It might take a while to complete this exercise the first time you do it.)

Using the DSMON report, for each APF-authorized library, do the following:

1. Under the RACF INDICATED column for each APF data set, it should say N (No). If it says Y (Yes), then the data set is protected by a RACF discrete profile. You should take steps to change this to a RACF generic profile. For more information about RACF discrete profiles, refer to chapter 11, "Security Administration: Beyond the Basics."

2. Under the RACF PROTECTED column, if a library is flagged as "not found" (NF), it means this library is marked as APF-authorized, but the report

could not find it using the normal catalog search. There might be a security exposure. Resolve the issue with your system programmers.

3. Look under the RACF PROTECTED column for each APF data set. It should say Y (Yes); this means there is RACF protection for this APF data set. If it says N (No), then the data set is not protected by RACF. Create a new profile to protect the data set.

   Even if the library is protected, this merely means there is a RACF profile covering it. It does not mean that the profile is appropriate. For an APF-authorized library, any generic profile is not good enough. You should create a separate "fully-qualified" generic profile for each of your APF-authorized libraries. For more information about fully-qualified generic profiles, refer to chapter 11.

4. Ensure that the universal access (UACC) is NONE. If the universal access is READ, make it NONE and add the general access ID(*) READ in the access list of the profile. A universal access of UPDATE, CONTROL, or ALTER is unacceptable—you are exposed to considerable security risks. You should change it to NONE, but of course only after you have taken precautions to make sure legitimate users have been added to the access lists, so they will continue to have access. For a discussion of universal access versus general access, refer also to chapter 11.

5. Go through the access list of the profile to make sure it has only system programmers, and possibly one or two batch IDs, having anything more than READ access.

6. Work with your system programmers to make sure the APF authorization for the library is required and still valid. Software products might have been removed or retired, or libraries might belong to older releases of software products, making them obsolete. If that is the case, have the system programmers remove the APF-authorized status of the library.

These steps make up a one-time exercise that will ensure appropriate protection for all your APF-authorized libraries. However, to keep it that way, you need to do the following on an ongoing basis:

1. Implement a process to add new APF-authorized libraries properly, after creating a fully-qualified generic profile.

2. Implement a process to remove APF-authorized libraries when they are no longer needed. This should include removing the individual RACF profile.

3. Make changes to members of APF-authorized libraries only after management approval.

4. Revalidate your APF-authorized libraries periodically. Keep them to a minimum. Ask for justification and approval for each new one.

5. Pay particular attention to security violations against APF-authorized libraries.

6. Many vendor products you purchase might require APF-authorized libraries. Make sure you trust the vendor before adding APF-authorized libraries to your existing list.

Summary

APF-authorized libraries are one of those security "back doors" that organizations often neglect to close properly. This makes it easy for unauthorized users to gain access to an organization's business assets.

Good security for APF-authorized libraries comes at a price, but in the end, the benefits far outweigh the costs.

13

The System Management Facility (SMF)

System Management Facility (SMF) data sets contain SMF records, which hold logs and audit trails of many of the events occurring on the mainframe. These logs include all security events that the installation has specified to be logged. Examples include security violations, logon failures, and activities of users with special privileges.

That's not all, however. The SMF records also include logs for non-security related activities, such as performance monitoring activities and computer usage information. To differentiate the various records, the SMF record "type" is used. SMF record types 30, 80, 81, and 83 are reserved for security-related events and activities. For more information about this topic, refer to chapter 4, "Security Event Logging and Auditing."

There are many uses of SMF records:

- When fraudulent activity is suspected, reports are run against the SMF records to find out who did what.

- Performance and capacity planning experts use these records to measure mainframe usage, and to find out when the next hardware upgrade will be required.

- The auditors, as part of their periodic audit, might ask you to provide proof of who accessed some important data set, such as the company's payroll master file.

For all these reasons, SMF records are retained for many years, and not just for security purposes, but for legal and other reasons as well.

What Is the Risk?

Even though the z/OS operating system provides the SMF record-gathering facility, it is up to the installation to specify which records are collected. You must ensure you are collecting all SMF record types your company requires.

If you do not collect the right SMF records, your company might be in violation of industry best practices, not to mention compliance and legal obligations.

In addition, the data sets holding these SMF records must be protected with proper security. Otherwise, unauthorized users might tamper with these records for various reasons, including covering up fraudulent activities.

Even reading these data sets carries a significant risk and should not be allowed. The average user does not need to know which user IDs have special powers or when a certain tax file was updated.

How Do You Mitigate This Risk?

Follow these steps to mitigate the risk:

1. The system parameter library SYS1.PARMLIB or its equivalent specifies which SMF records are to be collected at your installation. (Talk to your system programmers to find out your installation-specific name of this library.)

The member name is SMFPRM*xx*, where *xx* is installation-specific. At a minimum, ensure this member includes the security-related records (types 30, 80, 81, and 83). Discuss with management what other non-security record types are required for your company, and make sure they are also indicated in this member as records to be collected.

Once you have the complete list of record types your installation relies on, ensure no changes are made to the member SMFPRM*xx* without management approval.

2. You need to secure SMF data sets with appropriate RACF profiles. The SMF records are written continuously, in real-time, to SMF data sets SYS1.MAN*x*, where *x* is a number. First, therefore, you need to protect these data sets with the generic profile SYS1.MAN*.**.

   There are other SMF data sets as well. As the real-time SMF data sets are filled, they are periodically dumped (copied) to archival data sets whose names are installation-defined. Find out from the system programmers the names of the installation-specified data sets that contain copies of SMF data, and protect those, too, as follows:

   a. For all RACF profiles protecting SMF data, ensure the profiles have universal access of NONE.

   b. It is reasonable to grant READ access to system programmers and security administrators, but to nobody else.

   c. UPDATE, CONTROL, or ALTER access should be granted only to one or two batch IDs.

3. Make sure you retain SMF records for many years, depending on your company's business, legal, and other requirements. Some companies keep SMF records for seven years, others for even longer periods. It is best to separate out the security-related records from the rest.

4. Organize your historical SMF records in "generation data groups" (GDGs) to assist you in quickly retrieving security logs when needed. The following are suggested GDG names and retention cycles:

    a. Daily records in GDG: HLQ.SMF.DAILY—the past seven days

    b. Weekly records in GDG: HLQ.SMF.WEEKLY—the past four weeks

    c. Monthly records in GDG: HLQ.SMF.MONTHLY—the past twelve months

    d. Yearly records in GDG: HLQ.SMF.YEARLY—at least seven years

Summary

Do not neglect the collection, protection, and retention of your SMF records. They are required not only to run your business, but also for legal and compliance reasons.

14
Operating System Data Sets

T he z/OS operating system data sets require special attention. In the previous chapters, you have learned about some of the more important ones, such as APF-authorized libraries and SMF data sets. There are many more, and we shall discuss them here.

System Parameter Libraries

System parameter libraries contain specifications (parameters) that are used during an initial program load (IPL) of the mainframe. These include the following:

- SYS1.PARMLIB, which contains system IPL parameters

- SYS1.PROCLIB, which contains important started procedures, such as JES2

- JES parameter libraries

- SYS1.VTAMLST, which contains VTAM® parameters

Typically, but not always, these important libraries have a high-level qualifier that begins with SYS (for example, SYS1). Some of these libraries have installation-specific names. To find out all of your system parameter libraries, talk to your system programmers.

What Is the Risk?

If these parameters are modified incorrectly, the system might not be able to come up during the next IPL. Even if the system starts, it might not start properly and might cause service disruptions and partial system failures.

The company might experience system "down-time," which can be very costly in financial terms. What is even worse, the fact that your system will not come up during the next IPL will go unnoticed for a long time, since these days, many weeks (or even months) might go by without an IPL.

For these reasons, you should take special care to protect all data sets containing these high-value parameters.

How Do You Mitigate This Risk?

You can take several steps to mitigate the risk of inappropriate changes to system parameter libraries:

1. Ensure there are fully-qualified generic RACF profiles covering them. For more information about this topic, refer to chapter 11, "Security Administration: Beyond the Basics."

2. Ensure that the universal access (UACC) to these profiles is NONE or READ. Only system programmers and batch IDs should have UPDATE or higher access.

3. Implement change-control procedures to make sure there is management approval for all changes to these libraries, even when authorized users make such changes.

System Catalogs

The z/OS catalogs are like the table of contents for all of the installation's data. They contain pointers to actual data on disks and tape cartridges.

There are two types of catalogs: the master catalog and user catalogs. While there is only one master catalog, there can be several user catalogs. The user catalogs help to improve system performance by distributing catalog searches among the various catalogs.

What Is the Risk?

If any of these catalogs is corrupted, the installation might, at a minimum, suffer service disruptions. Another, more likely scenario is that some of the installation data will not be available to users, and this can have a serious impact on the business. In the worst case, the entire operating system might fail to start during the next IPL. Therefore, protecting all z/OS system catalogs is of vital importance.

How Do You Mitigate This Risk?

The first task to mitigating this risk is finding out all the names of the z/OS catalogs. To do this, run the Data Security Monitor (DSMON) Selected Data Sets report. For more information about DSMON, refer to chapter 3, "The Data Security Monitor (DSMON)."

Here is a partial sample DSMON Selected Data Sets report:

```
                        SELECTED DATA SETS REPORT

                        VOLUME        SELECTION

DATA SET NAME           SERIAL        CRITERION

-------------------------------------------------------------------

SYS1.MSTRCAT            DISK001       MASTER CATALOG

SYS1.USER.CATALOG1      DISK991       USER CATALOG

                                                        continued
```

```
UCAT.TSO.USER.CATALOG      DISKTSO     USER CATALOG

- - - - - -                - - - -     - - - - - - - -

UCAT.PROD.USER.CATALOG     DISKPRD     USER CATALOG
```

All data sets listed in this report should be protected by RACF profiles.

You need to define a fully-qualified generic profile for the master catalog. For more information, refer to chapter 11. Depending on your data set naming standards, the user catalogs might or might not need fully-qualified generic profiles. You might be able to have a generic profile, such as USER.CAT*.**.

Next, for the master catalog, ensure the universal access is NONE. Grant READ access to everyone using the ID(*) READ specification in the access list. Users might not be aware that they are reading this catalog when they refer to any cataloged data set at the installation. Grant UPDATE (or higher) access to system programmers and one or two batch IDs.

For user catalogs, the universal access should be NONE. Grant CONTROL access to everyone using the ID(*) CONTROL specification in the access list. This is required, as the user catalogs get updated whenever users create new data sets or delete old ones. Grant ALTER access only to system programmers and one or two batch IDs.

Assorted Operating System Data Sets

This assorted list should include any z/OS operating system data sets not covered so far; all system-critical data sets, catalogs, and databases belonging to VTAM, DB2, CICS and IMS; and any other critical software product data sets you might have that, if left unattended, would result in serious computer down-time and therefore incur a financial loss.

All these data sets will likely have a high-level qualifier such as SYS1, SYS2, or SYS3. The installation might also have designated other high-level qualifiers, apart from these. Check with the system programmers to find out all high-level qualifiers that are reserved for these operating system data sets.

What Is the Risk?

Since we are talking about a varied collection of data sets, the risks are also varied. In general, if the operating system data sets at the installation are compromised in any way, the system might not come up properly the next time you start it. There might be system down-time, and you might have system integrity problems.

How Do You Mitigate This Risk?

You should build appropriate RACF profiles to protect these assorted operating system data sets. For example, SYS1.** can cover all data sets beginning with SYS1, and so on. Ensure all these profiles have universal access of NONE. Granting READ access to everyone is acceptable, but only system programmers and a couple of batch IDs should have UPDATE access or higher.

Also, you should implement change-management standards and controls to make sure changes to these data sets are done only after management approval. Lastly, conduct a periodic review of these RACF profiles to ensure that security controls are in place.

Summary

In general, operating system data sets lie in the background and do not clamor for your attention. That does not mean they are unimportant, however. In fact, when one of them is corrupted, the entire computer installation might suffer in a number of ways.

15

RACF Databases

RACF databases contain all the security definitions that have been put in place by the security department. The RACF databases are, in fact, an integral part of the z/OS operating system.

There is the primary RACF database, and its backup version. If the primary database is corrupted for any reason, then the backup version can be used.

Only on rare occasions would you need to switch RACF databases from the primary to the backup version. However, in case you have to switch, RACF provides the RVARY operator command in order to do this. The RVARY command is password-protected to prevent its misuse.

What Is the Risk?

First, there is the risk of RACF database corruption. If this were to happen, then the installation's security and integrity would be at stake. In addition, if the RACF databases were corrupted, the operating system might not start properly at the next IPL. Your installation might suffer computer down-time.

The second risk is unauthorized users reading or copying information from RACF databases. The average user should not be able to find out how your security is protected via RACF.

Lastly, although the RVARY command is password-protected, when RACF is installed, default passwords for the RVARY command are in effect. These default passwords are documented in publicly available places such as IBM manuals; hence, they are readily available to unauthorized individuals.

How Do You Mitigate This Risk?

To mitigate the risk to your RACF databases, you need to do the following, discussed in more detail in the rest of this chapter:

1. Protect the RACF databases by defining fully-qualified generic profiles for them.

2. Protect all the unload RACF data sets that you are creating regularly from the RACF databases.

3. Change the password for the RVARY command from the default to an installation-defined one. You need to do this every time you install a new version of RACF.

Step 1: Protect the RACF Databases

You need to protect the RACF databases by defining fully-qualified generic profiles for the RACF databases. To find the names of your RACF databases, enter the following command:

```
RVARY LIST
```

The results will show you both the primary and backup RACF database names:

```
                          RACF DATABASE STATUS:

ACTIVE   USE    NUMBER   VOLUME   DATA SET

------   ---    ------   ------   -------

 YES     PRIM     1      SYSVOL   SYS1.RACF.PRIMARY.DATABASE

 YES     BACK     1      SYSRES   SYS1.RACF.BACKUP.DATABASE
```

After you have the RACF database names, you need to define fully-qualified generic profiles for them. For more information, refer to chapter 11, "Security Administration: Beyond the Basics." Once you have the appropriate profiles defined, ensure you have the following controls:

- Only started procedures and batch IDs may have UPDATE or higher permission to these data sets.

- System programmers and security administrators may have READ access.

- The universal access must be NONE, and no other users should be in the access lists for these profiles.

Step 2: Protect All the Unload RACF Data Sets

You need to protect all the *unload* RACF data sets (sometimes referred to as RACF *flat files*) that you are creating regularly from the RACF databases. The names of these RACF flat files are installation-dependent. Find these out from your system programmers.

Create appropriate profiles covering these data sets, and ensure you have RACF protection as follows:

- The universal access should be NONE.

- Only the security administrators and the system programmers should have READ access.

- Only one or two batch IDs should have ALTER access.

Step 3: Change the Password for the RVARY Command

You need to change the password for the RVARY command from the default password to an installation-defined one that only authorized users know. Find out whether this is already done. If you enter the SETROPTS LIST command and find the following, you have not changed the default passwords after installing RACF:

```
DEFAULT RVARY PASSWORD IS IN EFFECT FOR THE SWITCH FUNCTION.

DEFAULT RVARY PASSWORD IS IN EFFECT FOR THE STATUS FUNCTION.
```

Change the default passwords using this command:

```
SETROPTS RVARYPW(SWITCH(your-switch-pw) STATUS(your-status-pw))
```

Now enter the SETROPTS LIST command again. You should see the following:

```
INSTALLATION DEFINED RVARY PASSWORD IS IN EFFECT FOR THE SWITCH FUNCTION.

INSTALLATION DEFINED RVARY PASSWORD IS IN EFFECT FOR THE STATUS FUNCTION.
```

Once you have changed the default passwords, make sure you store them in a secure place, to be used in emergency situations requiring changes to the RACF databases.

Summary

In most cases, the RACF databases work fine, as designed. However, it is up to you to take precautions to ensure their continued uninterrupted operation. The RACF unload data sets, too, need proper protection because they contain important security information.

✓ How Secure Is *Your* Installation?

Have you changed the default passwords for the RVARY command? If you have not, your installation is at considerable risk. You should take immediate steps to change the default passwords.

16
RACF Exits

A RACF exit is an optional facility provided in RACF to perform special RACF processing, above and beyond what is offered in standard RACF. RACF exits can overrule decisions made by standard RACF processing. They provide a means for an installation to tailor RACF processing to suit its own unique needs.

Not all installations have special processing requirements. For most, the standard RACF facilities provided are sufficient. In that case, the question of implementing RACF exits does not arise. Some installations, however, need non-standard security features, in which case they would need to implement RACF exits. Here are two examples:

- The installation wants to implement more stringent password controls, above and beyond what RACF provides.

- The installation wants to pre-process (or post-process) the decision taken by RACF, whether to grant or deny an access.

While IBM provides the RACF exit provision, it is up to the installation to write and implement these exits.

What Is the Risk?

RACF exits are double-edged swords. Used properly, they can enhance security at an installation. If they are misused or if proper safeguards are not instituted, however, then the repercussions can be costly. For example, the RACF pre-processing and post-processing exits mentioned above can override most of the controls you have put in place by means of RACF profiles.

Sometimes RACF exits are written to provide a short-term solution to a problem, but when the need is gone, they might still remain in place.

The biggest problem with RACF exits is that, if they are not properly implemented, they can give you a false sense of security. You might look at your RACF profiles and think your business data is adequately protected, while unknown to you, the RACF exits could be negating some or all aspects of your security specifications.

All the security you've defined in RACF profiles might mean nothing if an exit is programmed to bypass some aspect of security-checking.

Exits are usually written by system programmers in Assembler language, a language not well-known to security practitioners. Exits are also maintained by system programmers. This often means that the security department is left out of the loop when it comes to RACF exits.

How Do You Mitigate This Risk?

To mitigate this risk, you first need to find out whether your installation has any RACF exits in place. To do this, run the DSMON RACF Exits report. For more information about DSMON, refer to chapter 3, "The Data Security Monitor (DSMON)."

Here is a partial sample DSMON RACF Exits report:

```
                        RACF EXITS REPORT

EXIT MODULE             MODULE

NAME                    LENGTH


-----------------------------------------------------------------

ICHCNX00                8FB
```

Here we see that the exit ICHNX00 is in place.

If you find any RACF exits in this report, you need to do the following for each exit to mitigate the risk factors:

1. Find out from the system programmers what the exit does. Make sure it is in line with corporate security policy and practices.

2. Periodically re-evaluate the need for having the exit. Ask yourself whether the exit is still relevant. It is possible that at one time it played a useful security role, but now the functions provided by it are available in standard RACF. The exit might have outlived its usefulness.

   For example, you might find that some of the stringent password controls your installation requires were not available by normal RACF means at one time. So, your installation might have written an exit to provide those additional features. Those features might now be available in RACF, however, making the exit obsolete.

   Another possibility is that an exit might have been meant to be on the system temporarily, but it is still in place. As an example, if the installation has converted from some other security software to RACF, the installation might have had to implement a temporary bypass to make security work under RACF. Over time, the staff might have overlooked re-examining the temporary aspect of this exit, and you might still have it. In such cases, removing this exit will remove the risk associated with its misuse.

3. If the exit is relevant, periodically compare the length, or "size," of the exit between two runs of the DSMON report to ensure that the module length hasn't changed without your knowledge. A change in the module length generally indicates the exit has changed. That is why the report above shows the length. Note that the length is given in hexadecimal.

4. Make sure management is aware of what is modified (or enhanced) over and above what RACF provides.

5. Document what the exit does. Make sure changes to the exit are made only after management approval.

Summary

Ideally, you should not have any RACF exits in place. Try to implement whatever security you desire using RACF's normal capabilities. RACF exits, once they are entrenched, are difficult to remove. It is best not to introduce them in the first place. If you must have them, however, do not neglect to mitigate their risk factors, as discussed in this chapter.

✓ How Secure Is *Your* Installation?

• Look at your installation's DSMON report. Do you see any RACF exits in place? If so, do you know what they do?

• Do you see the RACF preprocessing exit ICHRIX01, or the post-processing exit ICHRCX02 or ICHRIX02? If so, pay particular attention to what exactly they do, as these can override the normal decisions RACF takes on whether to allow access to a resource.

17

System Exits

In addition to the RACF exits mentioned in the previous chapter, there are other system exits as well. The idea is the same: they allow special processing that the standard operating system might not provide.

While RACF exits modify the behavior of standard RACF processing, system exits modify the behavior of other operating system functions that have nothing to do with security.

Some of the system exits are as follows:

- *SMF exits*—These exits can enable the installation to implement reporting and billing systems for system work done by various users and by batch jobs.

- *JES exits*—These exits modify the way jobs are run on the system. Typically, they perform functions such as changing job priorities and enforcing some of the installation's batch processing standards.

What Is the Risk?

System exits do not modify RACF processing, so one would think they would not be a security threat. However, they modify other operating system functions that could potentially bypass RACF and system security.

If unauthorized code were to creep into the system exits, your installation's security could easily be compromised. Your installation would be at risk from operating system integrity issues, including unintended system down-time. So, protecting system exits is as important as protecting RACF exits.

How Do You Mitigate This Risk?

To mitigate this risk, you first need to find out whether you have system exits in place. Unfortunately, unlike RACF exits, DSMON does not report on system exits.

The only way to find out whether you have system exits is by talking to your system programmers. Find out from them what system exits, if any, are in place and what they do. The same points mentioned for mitigating the risk of RACF exits in the previous chapter also apply here.

For each system exit, do the following:

1. Periodically re-evaluate the need for having each exit.

2. Make sure management is aware of what is modified (or enhanced) over and above what the operating system provides.

3. Document what the exit does. Make sure changes to it are made only after management approval.

Summary

The same rules of thumb discussed for RACF exits in the previous chapter apply to system exits, as well:

- Try to avoid their use.

- If you must have them, mitigate the risk factors as described in this chapter.

✓ How Secure Is *Your* Installation?

Do you have any system exits in place at your installation? Do you know what they do? How are you protecting these exits and making sure they are designed to perform management-approved functions only?

18
Started Procedures

Started procedures were called "started tasks" at one time. Even today, some people refer to them by their old name. They reside in the installation's procedure libraries. In addition to the IBM-supplied procedure library named SYS1.PROCLIB, the installation might have defined additional procedure libraries that contain started procedures.

Started procedures are processes or "tasks" performing functions that are usually, but not always, associated with the operating system. They are roughly equivalent to daemons in the UNIX operating system.

RACF requires that all started procedures be associated with a RACF user ID for authentication and access-checking purposes. A started procedure can also have the TRUSTED or the PRIVILEGED attribute, both of them very powerful, and both only applicable to started procedures.

There is a RACF class called STARTED where you define all started procedures. This class is relatively new to RACF. Prior to that, installations used a load module called the ICHRIN03 table to define started procedures. In fact, there might still be some installations using this old method. The way it works is, if a started procedure is not found in the STARTED class, then the ICHRIN03 table is checked.

The introduction of the STARTED class to RACF was a big benefit to security administrators because there were some issues with the previous method. First, the ICHRIN03 table needed to be reinstalled every time a started procedure was added, deleted, or changed. This usually required a system programmer's involvement. Moreover, the change would be effective only after the next IPL of the system. The STARTED class did away with these rather annoying restrictions. The side benefits of the STARTED class are that it is now easier to administer security for started procedures, and it is easier to audit them as well.

What Is the Risk?

Many started procedures have the TRUSTED or PRIVILEGED attribute assigned to them. Both of these attributes allow the started procedure to access any resource (data sets, transactions, and any other resource) defined at your installation. The only difference between the two attributes is that the TRUSTED attribute will allow you to enable logging to SMF of all the accesses that are granted, whereas the PRIVILEGED attribute will not. For more information about SMF, refer to chapter 13, "The System Management Facility (SMF)."

Started procedures having these powerful attributes can bypass security safeguards at your installation, so the company's data integrity might be at risk. In the case of the PRIVILEGED attribute, the accesses will not even be recorded to SMF.

Many started procedures, such as JES2, require these special powers, since they are an integral part of the operating system. However, some questionable started procedures that have nothing to do with the operating system might have been assigned one of these powerful privileges. That is the risk you need to mitigate.

How Do You Mitigate This Risk?

Since TRUSTED and PRIVILEGED attributes allow a started procedure to access all information without any RACF checking, you should make sure these attributes are assigned only if there is justification, and only after management approval.

To find any started procedures having these attributes, run the DSMON RACF Started Procedures Table reports. For more information about DSMON, refer to chapter 3, "The Data Security Monitor (DSMON)."

Two reports are generated, one for entries in the STARTED class and one for entries in the module ICHRIN03. Here is a (partial) sample of the first RACF Started Procedures Table report:

```
R A C F   S T A R T E D   P R O C E D U R E S   T A B L E   R E P O R T

FROM PROFILES IN THE STARTED CLASS:

-------------------------------------------------------------------

PROFILE              ASSOCIATED  ASSOCIATED

NAME                 USER        GROUP      PRIVILEGED  TRUSTED  TRACE

-------------------------------------------------------------------

JES2.*  (G)          STCUSER     SYS1       YES         NO       NO

CICS.*  (G)          CUSER1      SYS3       NO          NO       NO

ZEKE.*  (G)          STCUSR      SYS1       NO          YES      NO. .

. . .

. . .
```

Here is a (partial) sample of the second report:

```
R A C F   S T A R T E D   P R O C E D U R E S   T A B L E   R E P O R T

FROM THE STARTED PROCEDURES TABLE (ICHRIN03):

----------------------------------------------------------------------

PROCEDURE        ASSOCIATED        ASSOCIATED

NAME             USER              GROUP          PRIVILEGED      TRUSTED

----------------------------------------------------------------------

JES2             STCUSER           SYS1           NO              YES

VTAM             STCUSER           SYS2           NO              YES

. . .

. . .
```

For each started procedure in these reports, work with your system
programmers on the following:

1. Ensure that the started procedure exists in one of the procedure libraries
    at your installation. If it does not exist, then consider removing the
    started procedure profile entry from the RACF STARTED class or from the
    ICHRIN03 table.

2. Look at the "TRUSTED" and "PRIVILEGED" columns in these reports. If
    the started procedure has either the TRUSTED or the PRIVILEGED attribute
    assigned to it, then review the need to have this powerful capability.

3. If the TRUSTED or PRIVILEGED attribute is required, then have management
    sign off on this requirement.

On an ongoing basis, do the following:

1. Implement stringent change-management controls so that changes made to the contents of all procedure libraries are approved by management.

2. Periodically revisit all started procedures and go through the above exercise.

Summary

The main point about started procedures is that they might have been assigned one of the special attributes, TRUSTED or PRIVILEGED. If that is the case, this might entail a security risk. Another point you need to understand is that there are two places where started procedures might reside: the STARTED class (preferred) and the ICHRIN03 table (obsolete, but still supported by IBM).

✓ How Secure Is *Your* Installation?

-   How many started procedures do you have that have either the PRIVILEGED or the TRUSTED attribute? Are they all justified?

-   Do you have entries in the ICHRIN03 table? Can you justify having them?

19

Tape Bypass Label Processing (BLP)

T he "label" in bypass label processing (BLP) refers to the tape label, so BLP applies only to data security for tapes or tape cartridges.

In security terms, there are two ways to access data on tape: either by using *standard* label processing or by using *bypass* label processing, or BLP. Standard label processing is the normal (and preferred) method. This type of processing invokes RACF security. The data set name found on the tape label is used to validate the access request. There are no additional security issues with this method.

What Is the Risk?

Security issues arise when someone uses the BLP method for accessing tape data. To understand the security exposure, it is important to see how data is stored on tapes and how it is processed.

Tape data set processing is different from DASD, or disk data set, processing. Unlike disks, tape cartridges do not have a VTOC (Volume Table of Contents). Instead, they have tape labels interspersed with data sets, like this:

Label 1	Data set 1	Label 2	Data set 2	. . . .

Tape labels contain the data set name and other information about the data set that follows the tape label. There can be multiple pairs of labels and data sets on a single tape.

Bypass label processing is the "abnormal" way to process a tape data set. As the term implies, you are asking the system to forego the processing of the tape label and go directly to the data. If the label is not processed, how can RACF do its authorization checking? This is abnormal, indeed. Essentially, there is no RACF protection for tape data sets accessed via the BLP facility.

You might wonder, if BLP is so risky, why allow it in the first place? The answer is, there are times when you have to use BLP. Consider the following scenarios:

- The tape label has become unreadable, so standard label processing will not work. The only option is to read and copy the data that follows the tape label, by bypassing the label.

- Your installation might have received what is termed a "foreign tape"—tape from another installation, where the data set name on the tape label might be unknown or wrong. Data centers often send and receive tapes for business reasons. The only way to read this tape data set is by bypassing standard label processing.

- Even if you know the data set name on a foreign tape label, this data set might not follow your installation's naming standards. Therefore, you might not have a RACF profile covering that data set. Instead of building a temporary RACF profile, a better way to read the tape might be to bypass the tape label.

How Do You Mitigate This Risk?

If BLP capability is misused, unauthorized users will be able to read tape data, creating a security exposure.

To mitigate the risk of misuse (or abuse) of BLP, you need to control who can use BLP. RACF allows you to do this by utilizing the ICHBLP profile in the FACILITY class.

First, define the ICHBLP profile in the FACILITY class:

```
RDEFINE FACILITY ICHBLP OWNER(owner-name) UACC(NONE)
```

Then, use the PERMIT command to grant BLP access:

```
PERMIT ICHBLP CLASS(FACILITY) ID(user1,user9) ACCESS(READ)
```

Make sure you allow only system programmers and computer console operators the BLP capability. Even better, allow only a batch ID to have this access, and then allow system programmers and operators surrogate access to this batch ID.

Periodically review all users who have BLP capability.

Summary

BLP is a security risk for business data residing on tape cartridges. Your job as the security practitioner is to minimize the number of users who can use BLP.

20

The SYS1.UADS Data Set

Even a paranoid can have enemies.
—Henry Kissinger

It might seem odd to devote an entire chapter to a single operating system data set. This is necessary, however, for this data set was at one time providing total security for TSO. It now plays a minor, yet noteworthy, role.

SYS1.UADS is a peculiar name for a data set. ("UADS" stands for User Attribute Data Set.) On the surface, it appears to have no bearing on security, but it still plays an important security role in some circumstances.

The SYS1.UADS data set, which is a partitioned data set (PDS), exists in all z/OS (or MVS or OS/390) installations. This data set is an integral part of the operating system. Many security administrators are not aware of its existence, much less the role it plays in security. Even today, SYS1.UADS works with RACF to provide some security. Admittedly, it only comes into play when logging onto TSO, but this in itself is significant.

We will first look at SYS1.UADS from a historical perspective, then see how it works in conjunction with RACF, and finally, list some recommendations on maintaining this important data set so TSO security is not compromised.

A Brief History of SYS1.UADS

The origins of SYS1.UADS date back to pre-RACF days. In other words, there was SYS1.UADS even when there was no RACF.

In pre-RACF days, the data set was used to control access to TSO, by authenticating user IDs and passwords for TSO users. It also validated the use of TSO resources such as account numbers, region size, and logon procedure names. In this sense, SYS1.UADS played a small part of the present role of RACF.

There were several disadvantages, however, to using SYS1.UADS as the primary means of TSO security, including these:

- TSO passwords were stored in clear text! Any user with the TSO ACCOUNT authority could see other user IDs' passwords, leaving open the possibility of misuse.

- When users wanted to change their passwords, they had to go to someone with the TSO ACCOUNT authority to get them changed.

When IBM introduced RACF, it included the TSO security functions of the data set SYS1.UADS, minus these disadvantages. It was hoped that installations would move away from SYS1.UADS. IBM even provided conversion tools to move the security from SYS1.UADS to RACF. This would place all security in one central place, improve TSO security, and negate the need to maintain SYS1.UADS as a separate security vehicle.

So it would seem that with the advent of RACF, SYS1.UADS would become obsolete, and it would go down in history as the old method of administering TSO security. To a large extent, that has happened. Because of the inherent disadvantages of SYS1.UADS, most installations undertook the one-time task of converting TSO security to RACF.

However, in typical IBM fashion, the features of SYS1.UADS were not removed; rather, they were replaced with better methods. It was left up to the installations to use these better methods, by migrating information from SYS1.UADS into the RACF umbrella and deleting all the SYS1.UADS entries.

Although SYS1.UADS would still work, it is hard to imagine anyone would want to go to the trouble of maintaining all TSO information for all users in the data set SYS1.UADS and use that to validate TSO users. Most installations did the migration of TSO information from SYS1.UADS to RACF. Some might have forgotten to remove the old SYS1.UADS entries, however, leaving open a potential security exposure.

How SYS1.UADS Works with RACF

SYS1.UADS still works in conjunction with RACF. In RACF, the use of TSO is controlled by the TSO segment of the user ID profile. If the user ID has a TSO segment, the user can log onto TSO; otherwise, not. However, there are some exceptions.

Essentially, *if RACF is active*, and a user ID attempts to log onto TSO, then SYS1.UADS comes into play in one of these two situations:

1. If the user ID is defined to RACF but does not have a TSO segment, then SYS1.UADS is checked to see whether the user ID is defined to SYS1.UADS. If the user ID is defined there, then the TSO logon continues.

2. If the user ID is not defined to RACF, then SYS1.UADS is checked to see whether an entry for this user ID exists. If it does, then TSO logon continues.

In other words, SYS1.UADS is referenced in cases where appropriate TSO information is not found in RACF.

When RACF is inactive, SYS1.UADS assumes its old role as the security gate-keeper, and user IDs defined to it can log onto TSO. If a user tries to log onto TSO, the logon will succeed if the password and other TSO attributes specified at logon match with those found in the SYS1.UADS entry for that user ID.

This can be very useful in emergency situations, for it allows someone to log onto TSO even when RACF is not active. And most likely, TSO is typically what system programmers need to "fix" the problem of RACF not being active.

So we see that entries in SYS1.UADS can come in handy in emergency situations. Ideally, it should contain entries for the user IDs of system programmers who would need to fix the operating system when RACF is down. But all other entries in this data set should be removed.

✓ How Secure Is *Your* Installation?

If you want to see how your installation is faring in this regard, just browse SYS1.UADS and see how many entries you find. You should only find entries for the user IDs of system programmers and for the special user ID IBMUSER. If you find any other entries, you should delete them, taking care to migrate the TSO information to TSO segments of the appropriate user IDs.

Keeping SYS1.UADS Current

It is important to keep current the valid entries in SYS1.UADS and remove all invalid ones.

The TSO ACCOUNT command is used to administer and maintain the entries in the SYS1.UADS data set. With this TSO command, you can list, add, delete, and change user ID information in SYS1.UADS.

Do the following to keep SYS1.UADS current:

1. For emergency situations such as disaster recovery testing, you should define an entry in SYS1.UADS for each of your system programmers. It is recommended that you have an entry for the user ID IBMUSER also.

2. Assign appropriate passwords, and since they are in clear text, store them in a secure place. This will come in handy in emergency situations.

3. Delete all extraneous entries from SYS1.UADS to prevent compromising the system. Before you delete these user IDs, however, make sure you have

defined appropriate TSO segments for them. You never know if users were logging onto TSO by virtue of these supposedly obsolete SYS1.UADS entries!

4. Specify a TSO segment in RACF for valid SYS1.UADS entries (system programmers' user IDs). This will prevent information from SYS1.UADS being used when RACF is available.

5. Perform a periodic review of the SYS1.UADS data set to make sure there are no redundant entries, and that the TSO attributes specified for the system programmer user IDs are still valid.

6. Limit the number of people having access to the TSO ACCOUNT authority. It is very powerful and should be treated just as you would treat other powerful RACF authorities. Only system programmers and security practitioners should have the ability to use the ACCOUNT command. To see who has access to use this command at your installation, enter the following RACF command:

```
RLIST TSOAUTH ACCT ALL
```

The access list you get from this command will show you who has access.

7. Define a fully-qualified generic profile called SYS1.UADS, with universal access (UACC) of NONE. For more information, refer to chapter 11, "Security Administration: Beyond the Basics." Make sure you have only the system programmers and possibly security administrators in the access list of this profile. You do not want anyone snooping into this data set and finding out what entries are there. You never know how that information might be misused.

Summary

The SYS1.UADS data set was the old way of providing TSO security. However, as with many RACF features, the old methods have not been completely eliminated, and if you are not careful, SYS1.UADS can cause security and audit concerns.

21

The System Display and Search Facility (SDSF)

T he System Display and Search Facility (SDSF) is an IBM program product that allows you to do a number of things through TSO. It is most often used for viewing batch job status, job output, and the system log. The system log is useful to a security practitioner for viewing RACF violations and other messages to determine why a batch job failed.

What Is the Risk?

The vast majority of users use SDSF for "display" functions, which are relatively harmless. There is a small risk associated with allowing everyone to view the system log because, among other things, it contains RACF error messages of security violations. These are messages prefixed by ICH and IRR, indicating they are RACF messages.

The larger risk, however, is that SDSF allows authorized users to enter JES and z/OS operator commands. Essentially, through SDSF, they can have at their disposal the powers of a z/OS operator console. This capability introduces a considerable level of risk if not properly controlled.

Using operator commands, a user can potentially harm the system in any number of ways, including bringing it down altogether.

How Do You Mitigate This Risk?

To mitigate the risk factors, consider implementing "external" SDSF security, if you have not already done so.

SDSF security can be "internal" to SDSF or "externally" managed by RACF. For more discussion on internal and external security, refer to chapter 25, "Security Architecture."

When SDSF was first introduced, it had internal security only. Security definitions, specifying which user could do what, were stored in an assembler table. This table needed to be reinstalled every time a security change was required. Because this process was technical, security administrators played only a minor role in defining SDSF security. The system programmers did all the work of adding, deleting, and changing SDSF security requirements.

Later, IBM provided the RACF SDSF class to allow installations to move SDSF security to RACF. This is called external SDSF security.

Most installations have migrated their SDSF security to RACF, to allow security practitioners to administer SDSF features and to better control use of the product. However, not all installations have done this.

If SDSF security at your installation is internal, consider moving it to RACF (external security) to be better able to manage the riskier functions of SDSF. If for some reason you have internal SDSF security and want to keep it that way, then the system programmers are most likely controlling SDSF security. Find out from them who can issue operator commands via SDSF. The list of authorized users should include only the system programmers, and no one else. Work with the system programmers to ensure changes to the SDSF table are made only after management approval.

If your SDSF security is controlled by RACF, then use RACF profiles in the SDSF class to ensure only the system programmers have the ability to use z/OS and JES operator commands. The universal access on these profiles should be NONE.

To reduce the risk of unauthorized users viewing the system log, you should only grant SDSF's system log-viewing capability on a need-to-know basis.

Quiz 21.1 is designed to help you better understand the system log.

Quiz 21.1

1. The system log contains many system messages. From these, how do you find out which ones are related to RACF?

   Answer: All RACF messages are prefixed by ICH or IRR. This convention of designating special three-character codes is used for all software products, IBM or otherwise. It helps to differentiate messages from various software products.

2. How long is the system log retained?

   Answer: At most installations, the system log that you can view in SDSF is recycled daily, so that you can view only the day's log at the most. Most installations have a process of archiving this log and retaining it for several years. If you ever have a need to view the system log from the past, contact the system programmers. Usually, there are GDG data sets that store the system log on a daily, weekly, monthly, and even yearly basis.

22

The Program Properties Table (PPT)

The idea behind having the program properties table (PPT) as part of the operating system is an old one, going back to the earliest days of IBM mainframes. These days, though, very few people know the exact function of this table, much less pay attention to its contents. From a security standpoint, this table contains a list of programs supplied by IBM as part of the operating system that are authorized to "run in a system key" and thus are able to bypass system security controls.

What Is the Risk?

Because the programs contained in the PPT can bypass system security, there is the risk of an unauthorized program being added to the PPT. If this were to happen, this unauthorized program would be able to bypass all of the security controls you have put in place. The program then could do wide-ranging damage and even compromise system integrity.

How Do You Mitigate This Risk?

To mitigate this risk, the first thing you need to do is find out what entries are defined in your PPT. To do this, run the DSMON Program Properties Table report. For more information about DSMON, refer to chapter 3, "The Data Security Monitor (DSMON)."

Here is a partial sample Program Properties Table report:

```
P R O G R A M    P R O P E R T I E S    T A B L E    R E P O R T

PROGRAM          BYPASS PASSWORD           SYSTEM

NAME             PROTECTION                KEY

-----------------------------------------------------------------

ISTINM01         YES                       YES

IKTCAS00         NO                        YES

AHLGTF           NO                        YES

HHLGTF           NO                        YES

IHLGTF           NO                        YES

IEFIIC           NO                        YES

.  .  .
```

At most installations, this report will contain many entries. This is not a security risk in itself, since the operating system needs many of its programs in the PPT.

The second column shows whether the program can bypass password protection. This is less important nowadays, as very few data sets are still password-protected. The third column shows whether the program has the ability to run in a system key and, therefore, be able to bypass all security.

The first time you look into this report, you need to ensure that all its entries are valid ones. The best way to do this is to enlist the help of the system programmers. They will be able to verify each entry.

Once this is done, all you need to do is periodically run the report to make sure no new entries are showing up in it. If you see any new entries, again ask the system programmers to validate them.

Another way to mitigate the risk is to have a process in place whereby you run the report periodically and ask the system programmers to validate the entire contents of the PPT.

✓ How Secure Is *Your* Installation?

When was the last time you contacted the system programmers to confirm the validity of all entries in the PPT? You should do this periodically as a precautionary measure.

23

Special-Use Programs

The z/OS operating system includes a few utility programs that perform sensitive functions. These programs are meant to be used by authorized persons only, and for specific reasons only. Most often, system programmers and computer operators run them, in tightly controlled environments.

Examples of these utility programs include the following:

- IEHINITT—This program is capable of erasing tape data. Its legitimate purpose is for "initializing" or "formatting" new tape cartridges so programmers can read and write data on them. Computer operators use this program when new tape cartridges are brought in and, on rare occasions, when an existing tape cartridge needs to be reformatted for some technical reason.

- ICKDSF—This program is capable of erasing disk data. Its function is similar to the IEHINITT program, except this one works on disks. It is used when new disk volumes are added to the existing pool of disks at an installation, or when there is a need to erase all data on a disk, such as after some system testing.

- IMASPZAP—This program has many names; it is also known as AMASPZAP and SUPERZAP. In the past, it was often used to directly update "executable assembler load modules," either as a quick fix to a program or when the source code for the program was not available. These days, its legitimate use is questionable, but the program still exists as part of the operating system at many installations, for historical reasons.

In addition to these, your installation might even have non-IBM special-use programs, or even home-grown ones. You might not be aware of these programs, but system programmers quite often have a "toolkit" they use on special occasions or for special purposes.

What Is the Risk?

If these special programs are not properly guarded, unauthorized users might use them to alter or even destroy the installation's data. What's more, this would be done without the normal RACF data set profile checks.

How Do You Mitigate This Risk?

RACF offers the capability to control who can use programs, via the PROGRAM class. Use this class to define RACF profiles for all important operating system programs such as those mentioned above.

In most cases, only the system programmers, computer operators, and one or two batch IDs should have the ability to run these programs.

To mitigate the risk even further, you should conduct a periodic review and verification process to make sure only the right users are in the access lists.

Note: If you do not currently have the PROGRAM class active at your installation, be careful before activating it. Otherwise, there might be a negative impact on all programs running on the system. Initially, you should have a back-stop profile, "**" in this class, that allows general access to all users.

PART THREE

SECURITY INFRASTRUCTURE MATTERS

In this part, we will look at some areas not directly related to day-to-day security administration, but which play an important role in mainframe security. These issues are strategic in nature and help to build a security infrastructure that will facilitate better management of the other aspects of security discussed in this book.

If the installation has built a strong security foundation based on best industry practices and principles, then the task of securing and managing all business assets becomes that much easier.

24

Application and Batch ID Security

There are no secrets better kept than the secrets that everybody guesses.
—George Bernard Shaw

All corporations run batch jobs for several applications, usually at night. These applications are of varying degrees of importance. A payroll application, for example, would fall into the "very important" category. On the other hand, an application for employee "fun day" activities would be classified as less important.

The Production Support department is usually entrusted with scheduling and running these batch jobs, and with ensuring that all batch jobs complete successfully. The applications run under batch IDs, which have appropriate powers to update the corporation's business data.

Segregate Production from Non-Production

It is important to segregate production applications from other work, such as test and development, by assigning separate batch IDs for each type of work that is going to be carried out using that batch ID. For example, for the payroll application, there should be at least three batch IDs. Sample names for these three IDs might be something like these: PPAYROLL for production payroll jobs, TPAYROLL for test payroll jobs, and DPAYROLL for development payroll jobs. In this example, only the batch ID PPAYROLL would have access to update payroll production data. This allows for tighter security and audit controls to be placed around production data.

Batch IDs Must Not Share Application Data

In addition to ensuring that only production batch IDs update production data, it is important to ensure that all applications have their own unique batch IDs. Different applications may not share batch IDs. If they do, business application results might become corrupted, and it will be difficult to trace the problem. Each batch ID should only have permission to work within its own application boundaries.

For example, suppose there is another application batch ID called PINEVENT that is meant for production work for the inventory application. This batch ID should not have access to any other application data, such as payroll data.

Figure 24.1 shows three production applications with their own unique batch IDs. Their access rights are confined to their own application data.

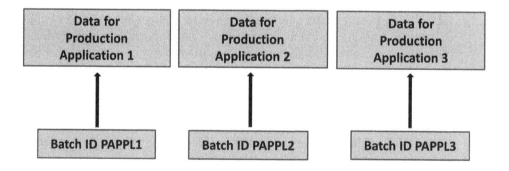

Figure 24.1: Batch IDs' access rights should be restricted to their own respective data.

Production JCL Must Not Refer to Personal Data Sets

If the production jobs are corrupted, then it follows that the business data will also be corrupted. One way to mitigate this risk is to not allow references to personal data sets in production JCL.

There are good reasons for this:

- Owners of personal data sets can modify them at will. This presents a significant security risk as these owners will have the ability to impact the integrity of production data.

- Personal data sets can be deleted easily, resulting in production batch failures.

- The owners of personal data sets can leave the company, raising ownership and accountability issues.

- The access lists protecting personal data sets are often lax, which might allow other users besides the owners to also negatively influence the integrity of production work.

The Production Support department should ensure that all JCL running production batch jobs goes through stringent change control to ensure there are no references to personal data sets.

Be Careful About SURROGAT Class Access

Most installations use the RACF SURROGAT class to allow some users access to the powers of batch IDs. When a user ID is allowed SURROGAT access to a batch ID, that user ID can submit a job that will run using the powers of the batch ID. Essentially, that user can do everything the batch ID is authorized to do. This carries with it considerable risk.

Make sure you grant SURROGAT access on a need-to-know basis only, and only after management approval. Otherwise, production data can be corrupted. Also, periodically review all user IDs getting SURROGAT batch access.

Some installations even have the restriction that only FIRECALL IDs may have surrogate access.

Note: The SURROGAT class profiles must not have unintended masking. For example, if you want to create a SURROGAT profile for batch ID PPAYROLL, then the profile should be PPAYROLL.SUBMIT, and not PPAYROLL.**. This is because the SURROGAT class is used for purposes other than to control batch surrogate access, and the masking, if not intended, can cause security exposures.

Restrict Direct Update Access to Production Data

There should be company policy that individual user IDs will not have direct UPDATE (or higher level) access to production data.

Updates to production data should be done only as follows:

- Using batch IDs and through batch jobs

- By means of transactions (using CICS, IMS, DB2, and so on)

This practice will ensure better controls and audit trails when you want to find out how certain production data got updated. It will also help ensure data integrity.

✓ How Secure Is *Your* Installation?

List all your profiles in the SURROGAT class. A simple way to do this is to use the following SEARCH command:

```
SEARCH MASK(**) CLASS(SURROGAT)
```

Do you have any profiles that have masking after the period following the batch ID, for example, BATCHID.**? If so, is this by design, or just an oversight?

25
Security Architecture

I think computer viruses should count as life. I think it says something about human nature that the only form of life we have created so far is purely destructive. We've created life in our own image.
—Stephen Hawking

It is important to have a strong architecture, or framework, on which the company's security policies and procedures are developed. From an overall perspective, how you manage your installation's security largely depends on two main factors:

- Are you using RACF (external security) for all or most of your security needs?

- How much control does the security department want to exert (centralized security) on the overall security in your organization?

Internal vs. External Security

Internal security and *external* security are mainframe concepts. To understand the difference between the two, we have to go back in time to when there was no RACF security, or very little RACF security. At that time, application products such as CICS were introduced. These products were designed to computerize and automate some of the manual processes. These products came complete with their own security controls, in their own databases. This was done to cater to installations that required security as a prerequisite. The security for CICS was internal to CICS, so the term *internal CICS security* was used.

Why did CICS use internal security? In those days, not all installations had RACF, so internal security was the better way to go.

As RACF security evolved, and as more and more installations had RACF in place, it became obvious that having all security for all software products under one umbrella was the better way to go. Not all installations were ready to make this potentially huge and risky switch, however. So CICS provided an option whereby you could either move CICS security definitions within RACF or maintain the status quo and let them continue to reside within CICS. If security was moved to RACF, it was referred to as *external CICS security*. Nowadays, external CICS security has become so widely accepted that CICS no longer offers the option to have internal security.

The same scenario unfolded with DB2: it came with its own internal security, but later gave the option to the installation to move the security to RACF. In the case of DB2, the option to have internal DB2 security is still there, and many installations still are using it.

Another product that supplied its own internal security was the System Display and Search Facility (SDSF). It, too, later provided the option to move security externally to RACF. For more details about SDSF, refer to chapter 21, "The System Display and Search Facility (SDSF)."

Although CICS, DB2, and SDSF are all IBM products, non-IBM software vendors also provided internal security for their products and later gave the

option to implement external security if the installation desired. OMEGAMON®
from Candle Corporation comes to mind, but there are several others.

Although more and more software vendors are now providing the option of
external security, there are some that still do not. It is in the company's best
interest, therefore, to have a policy that external security is a prerequisite
before making a software product purchase.

The Benefits of External (RACF) Security

If given a choice, an installation should always select external security over
internal security. Here are some of the benefits of external security:

- *Easy to administer*—When security is in one place, it is easy to administer
  the security definitions. There is one set of consistent commands to do the
  administration work.

- *Easy to interpret security definitions*—Since RACF provides a single,
  consistent interface for all security, it follows that external security will
  do away with product-specific definitions and rules that govern internal
  security.

- *Easy to audit*—Needless to say, auditors prefer external security for all
  security products. Having all security in one place makes their auditing
  job much easier.

- *Uniform security controls*—Because only the security administration
  group is handling security, the group will likely provide consistent
  security among all the various products.

- *Better accountability*—The security administration group is held
  accountable for all controls (or lack thereof), instead of many groups.
  Since the security group is in the sole business of securing corporate data,
  it follows that the group will be better accountable for its actions.

✓ **How Secure Is *Your* Installation?**

Find out from various sources, including talking to your system programmers and application developers, if there are any software products at your installation that still use internal security. If the answer is yes, ask yourself, is this justified?

Centralized Security or Decentralized Security?

In the previous section, we saw that putting all security (or as much of it as possible) within RACF is the best way to go. There are many advantages, and little or no negative impact.

The answer to a related issue is not so simple: Should your installation centralize all areas of security within one group, such as the security department, or should it let other departments manage some portion of the company's security?

The answer depends on two considerations:

- How big is your organization? Is it large enough to have specialized and skilled staff in the security department, who will be able to effectively manage security for such diverse areas as DB2, z/OS UNIX, digital certificates, IMS, and so on?

- How geographically dispersed is your organization? Does it operate on different continents? Is it across different time zones? Does it cross cultural boundaries? Are different languages spoken in some of the company's divisions?

The Advantages of Centralized Security

There are several advantages to centralized security:

- *Easier to audit*—The auditors have to go to only one place, and meet with only one group of people, to conduct an audit.

- *Easier to administer*—Security is easier to deal with when there is one set of people doing it. It is easy to discuss issues and resolve conflicts.

- *Uniform application*—When security is centralized, you can apply standards uniformly across all areas.

The Advantages of Decentralized Security

There are also a few advantages to decentralized security:

- *Niche security skills used*—Consider z/OS UNIX as an example. Unless the security department has a UNIX-specific person, it is very difficult to implement and administer z/OS UNIX security. On the other hand, someone from the UNIX group could easily make decisions about z/OS UNIX security.

- *Better communication*—In the case of companies that are geographically spread out, it is easier to have local groups manage, for example, password reset requests. They are more likely to understand the language and the culture and be able to monitor user password management.

Ultimately, for most corporations, the best answer may be a mixture of both centralized and decentralized security: you should centralize security functions where feasible, but hand them over to other groups and departments when skills are lacking or when there are problems of geography.

✓ How Secure Is *Your* Installation?

Are some of the security functions at your installation decentralized? If so, what is the rationale?

26

The RACF Unload Database

The RACF unload database, or the RACF "flat file" as it is sometimes called, is a term applied to a copy of the RACF database that contains "readable" RACF records of all security definitions at the installation. (The RACF database is in a format that is unreadable to all except RACF itself.)

The RACF unload database is created from the actual RACF database by an IBM-supplied program. This program will dump the RACF profile records from the RACF database into the RACF unload database.

Most installations have a process that creates the RACF flat file from the RACF database daily. This file is often used as input to various programs that produce customized security reports for the installation.

Since there are different types of RACF records, each record is "tagged" to denote its type. For example, all basic user profile records have a type code of 0200, basic group profile records have type 0100, and so on.

How It Was Done Before

We did not always have the luxury of the RACF unload database. Long ago, when RACF was in its infancy, there was no such thing as an unload database. To appreciate how useful the unload database is, we need to see how things were done before it was made available.

Security administrators in the past had to run RACF commands in batch mode to get a crude listing of the information they needed from the RACF database. For example, if they wanted to produce a list of all user IDs and the names of people associated with them, they issued the following RACF command in batch mode:

```
LISTUSER *
```

The list they got from this command was of course not in a nice, reportable format. So, they used some sort of a "post-processor," in the form of a CLIST or a REXX script, or even an SAS program that "massaged" the output from the LISTUSER command to produce a more readable report.

This is just a simple example. Some of the other tasks involved even more complicated procedures.

You can imagine how time-consuming this must have been! Not only did it waste the valuable time of a security professional, but this method also took its toll on RACF performance, as the RACF commands were run against the "live" RACF database. In the case of the LISTUSER command, if there were several thousand user IDs, as is the case at large organizations, the impact on performance would be significant every time this was done.

Another drawback of the old method was that it would work only so long as IBM did not change the format of the output from RACF commands. If the format changed, then the process would have to change also.

Creating the RACF Unload Database

To use the RACF unload database, you need to create it regularly from the actual RACF database. The following JCL will do it. You might have to change this to meet your installation's JCL standards:

```
//RACFUNLD EXEC PGM=IRRDBU00,PARM='NOLOCKINPUT'

//SYSPRINT DD SYSOUT=*

//INDD1    DD DSN=SYS1.RACF.BACKUP,DISP=SHR

//OUTDD    DD DSN=HLQ.RACF.DB.UNLOAD(+1),

//            DISP=(NEW,CATLG,DELETE),

//            SPACE=(CYL,(10,10),RLSE),RECFM=FB,LRECL=4096
```

Note that we are using the backup copy of the RACF database as input, and not the primary database, so as not to slow down RACF performance.

The Benefits of the RACF Unload Database

The RACF unload database offers these benefits:

- The database is in Physical Sequential (PS) format. Therefore, it is readable in a TSO ISPF session. As you will see later in this chapter, this can be useful at times.

- You can run programs written in various languages, including REXX and SAS, to produce reports. In addition, you can produce reports using the IBM programs DFSORT and ICETOOL.

- You can upload the entire unload database to a DB2 database for writing DB2 queries. IBM provides a sample of DB2 statements that can be used to load the RACF unload database to DB2. If you want to do this, refer to the member IRRADULD in SYS1.SAMPLIB.

- You can export the file to a personal computer and upload the records to a PC-based database, such as Microsoft Access®. You can then write PC-based queries to get your results.

The Uses of the RACF Unload Database

With the RACF unload database, you can produce all kinds of reports, either on an ad hoc basis or regularly.

You would want to write ad hoc reports to undertake a RACF cleanup project or to reorganize parts of your RACF database.

As for regular reports, there are many that you can produce easily. They would be handy "tools" in your RACF toolkit, and you can use them for audit and quality assurance purposes. For example, suppose you want to know how many user IDs have UID(0) specified in their OMVS segments. This is the "superuser" privilege in z/OS UNIX, and it gives its holders wide-ranging special powers.

The following SORT JCL and control statements will give you such a list. This code uses the unload database as input to DFSORT. You might have to change this to meet your installation's JCL standards:

```
//SORTSTEP   EXEC PGM=SORT,REGION=128K

//SORTLIB    DD   DSN=SYS1.SORTLIB,DISP=SHR

//SYSOUT     DD   DUMMY

//SORTIN     DD   DSN=RACF.UNLOAD.DATABASE(0),DISP=SHR

//SORTOUT    DD   DSN=HLQ.USERS.HAVING.UID0(JAN01),DISP=SHR

//SORTWK01 DD   UNIT=SYSDA,SPACE=(CYL,5)

//SORTWK02 DD   UNIT=SYSDA,SPACE=(CYL,5)

//SORTWK03 DD   UNIT=SYSDA,SPACE=(CYL,5)

//SYSIN      DD   *

SORT    FIELDS=(10,8,CH,A)

INCLUDE COND=(5,4,CH,EQ,C'0270',AND,19,10,CH,EQ,C'0000000000')
```

Similar DFSORT JCL can be used to produce these other reports:

- Data set and resource profiles in WARNING mode.

  This list is critical, since ideally, no profile should have WARNING mode. For more information about WARNING mode, refer to chapter 8, "WARNING Mode and Its Implications."

- A list of all user IDs, together with the names of owners (from the name field of the user ID profile) and the date they last used the system.

  Many installations like to have this list. It is used for reference purposes to quickly find out the name of the person having a particular user ID, or to see whether a particular user (name) has any RACF user ID. In addition, if the "name" field is missing, this list will bring it to your attention, and you can insert one. The name field in the user ID profile is quite often used by programs to determine whose user ID this is.

- All data set and resource profiles having universal access (UACC) higher than NONE, that is, READ, UPDATE, CONTROL, or ALTER.

  You might want to review this list to see whether universal access greater than NONE is justified.

- All data set and resource profiles containing the specification ID(*) in the access list.

  The asterisk denotes all users at the installation. If a RACF profile has ID(*) in the access list and the access is greater than READ, then you might want to review and justify it.

Getting Quick Answers Using TSO

There are times when you can simply use TSO's ISPF VIEW (or BROWSE or EDIT) function to come up with meaningful numbers from the unload database.

Example 1

The security manager in your company says, "Give me a rough idea of how many user IDs are using the mainframe system."

In the unload database, there is one type-200 record for every user ID. Knowing this, your task is easy. Use ISPF VIEW to display your latest version of the unload database. Then, enter the following commands:

```
EXCLUDE ALL

FIND "0200" 1 ALL
```

Figure 26.1 shows the results of these commands.

```
CPU1    YOUR.UNLOAD.DATABASE                                    1358  CHARS  '0200'

COMMAND ===> _____Scroll ===> CSR_

****** **************************** TOP OF DATA ********************************

------------------------------------------------------------- 5 Lines not Displayed

000006 0200 SMITH10 2010-05-20 GROUP3      NO   YES   NO   NO   NO      030

------------------------------------------------------------- 22 Lines not Displayed

000029 0200 MARY123 2010-05-20 GROUP3      NO   YES   NO   NO   NO      030

------------------------------------------------------------- 7 Lines not Displayed

000037 0200 GURU01  2010-05-20 GROUP3      NO   YES   NO   NO   NO      030

------
```

Figure 26.1: This is a partial view of results of the EXCLUDE *and* FIND
commands.

The number reported in the top-right corner by the FIND command (1358 in
Figure 26.1) is the total number of user IDs in your RACF database, because
there is one type-200 record for each user ID. These user ID records contain
information from the user ID profile. Starting in column 6, you see the user ID.

Note that it would be incorrect to assume that the number of user IDs you
find here is the number of "human" users of your system. Some of these
will be batch and other non-personal IDs. This method will give you a quick
"ball-park" figure, however, which is what the security manager wants in this
example.

Example 2

You want to conduct a review and validation of all your data set profiles (or
resource profiles). First, though, you want to get a quick idea of the size of this

project. That is, you want to know how many data set profiles and how many resource profiles you have in your RACF database.

There is one type-400 record for each data set profile and one type-500 record for each resource profile. Knowing this, you can "view" your latest copy of the unload database in a TSO ISPF session. Then, enter the following commands:

```
EXCLUDE ALL

FIND "0400" ALL 1

FIND "0500" ALL 1
```

The first FIND command will tell you how many data set profiles you have, and the second one will give you the count of your resource profiles.

Figure 26.2 shows the results of the first FIND command (data set profiles).

```
CPU1    YOUR.UNLOAD.DATABASE                                    3829  CHARS  '0400'

COMMAND ===> _____Scroll ===> CSR_

****** **************************** TOP OF DATA *****************************************
----------------------------------------------------------- 5675 Lines not Displayed

005676 0400 ACCT.MONTHLY.*.DATA.**                 YES     2009-08-12      ACCT
----------------------------------------------------------- 13 Lines not Displayed

005690 0400 PAYROLL.**.YEARLY.FILE                 YES     2010-03-05      PAYROLL
----------------------------------------------------------- 7 Lines not Displayed

005697 0400 ZOZU.SPECIAL.PROJECT.**                YES     2008-01-07      ZOZU
------
```

Figure 26.2: This is a partial view of the results for the total number of data set profiles.

The number reported in the top-right corner by the FIND command (3829 in Figure 26.2) is the total number of data set profiles at your installation.

Summary

The examples discussed here are only the tip of the iceberg. They show you only what can be done easily, using DFSORT and TSO. However, you can do more complicated extracting and security reporting from the unload database using REXX, SAS, or some other programming language.

When it comes to finding good uses of the RACF unload database, the sky is the limit!

27

Increasing Your Productivity

To go forward, you must backup.
—Cardinal rule of computing

As a security practitioner, you can achieve more by working smarter, not necessarily harder. First, however, you have to take a step back to see the big picture, and use better "tools" in order to do this. As Stephen Covey would say, you need to sharpen your saw.

Most organizations are facing budget constraints, and training dollars are hard to come by. Often, security practitioners are left to their own devices when it comes to training and development.

The suggestions in this chapter will help increase your productivity at your own pace.

Use REXX and CLISTs

The good thing about REXX and CLISTs is that these tools are already there for you to use, at no extra charge. Even simple REXX routines and CLISTs can increase your productivity. True, you have to learn how to use these tools, and you have to expend the initial cost. Once that is done, however, you will earn handsome dividends.

Many of the reports you need to manage enterprise security can be written in-house. When you write your own reports, they are already customized the way you want them.

It might take a while to be proficient in REXX, but it is a relatively easy language to start out with. And it is possible to produce useful reports with only a little knowledge of REXX.

For example, most installations produce a daily report that lists all user IDs in their RACF database, together with such details as the name of the person to whom the user ID belongs and the date the user ID was last used. This report can be produced with very little effort using REXX and the RACF unload database.

For more information about the RACF unload database, refer to chapter 26, "The RACF Unload Database."

Learn More About ISPF Edit Capabilities

Another powerful tool you have at your disposal is TSO's ISPF editor. It might seem that ISPF does not have much to do with security, but the ISPF editor is very useful in producing ad hoc security reports without much effort. All you need is knowledge of some of the important ISPF editor commands, such as EXCLUDE and FIND.

For example, suppose you have entered the RACF LISTUSER * command to get a list of all RACF user IDs at your installation. This list is not very readable because it has every detail about all the user IDs, so you want to filter it to see only the user IDs and their default groups. How do you do this?

Follow these steps to get your desired result:

1. Edit the data set containing the output from the LISTUSER * command.

2. Enter the ISPF command

    | EXCLUDE ALL |

    This command will exclude all lines from being displayed (although they are still there).

3. Enter two more commands. The first one will display all occurrences of the text "USER=":

    | FIND 'USER=' ALL |

    The second one will find all default groups:

    | FIND "DEFAULT-GROUP=" ALL |

4. Delete all the lines that are still excluded, using the following command:

    | DELETE ALL EXCLUDED |

5. Finally, enter the command SAVE (or PF3).

And you have your report. You might not have an aesthetically pleasing result, but you have an accurate list of all user IDs at your installation and their default groups. The report will look as follows:

```
USER=JOHNS10     NAME= JOHN SMITH    OWNER= GROUP82    CREATED=99.123

     DEFAULT-GROUP=DFLTGRP1  PASSDATE=00.000 PASS-INTERVAL=90

USER=MARY05      NAME= MARY BROWN    OWNER= GROUP123   CREATED=98.345

     DEFAULT-GROUP=DFLTGRP2  PASSDATE=00.000 PASS-INTERVAL=90

. . .
```

From this starting point, you can learn more about the capabilities of the ISPF editor and how it can help you in your security management tasks. If you want to see what edit commands are available to you, press the PF1 key in an ISPF edit session, and look for "EDIT commands." There is a wealth of information there.

Join Online User Groups

Online sites such as LinkedIn have user groups that are specifically meant for mainframe security practitioners. By joining these groups, you will not only learn more but also be able to network with other experts in the field.

There is an online discussion group specifically meant for RACF security practitioners using RACF. It's called RACF-L, and its URL is as follows:

http://www.listserv.uga.edu/archives/racf-l.html

By subscribing to RACF-L, you can learn at your own pace by "listening" to the various topics being discussed. If you want more challenges, you can even participate by replying to some of the issues. And, of course, you can post your own questions. There is nothing like help and advice from people who are actually doing the daily security administration work.

Find a Mentor

As the saying goes, if you want to know the road ahead, ask the person coming back. Is there anyone you know who has spent a lot of time doing mainframe security? Such a person would be ideal to guide you in your own journey.

In your workplace, you might have a non-mainframe person looking after UNIX security. While a UNIX course might be helpful, you can learn a lot of the practical aspects of UNIX security by engaging in discussion with your UNIX colleague. What's more, you can learn at your own pace, when you have the time.

In return, if the person wants to learn about mainframe security, you can show him or her the ropes. This way, you both learn. "Help and be helped"—that should be your mantra.

System programmers are another resource you can draw upon. It might not be appropriate to ask them how to install RACF or perform some other complicated process. However, if you ask them something like "How do I do this in ISPF?" they can usually point you in the right direction.

Use RACF Help Functions

There is a lot of knowledge right at your fingertips! It might sound trivial, but try typing the Help command in ISPF:

```
HELP ALTUSER
```

You will be surprised at how many optional keywords this command has. You can get help on any RACF command right from ISPF.

Use Online Manuals

Online manuals are a useful source of learning. The fact that you can find information using keyword searches makes this an important resource. In contrast, back in the days when everything was in hardcover manuals, you had to scan the table of contents, sometimes of several manuals, before finding what you were looking for.

IBM RACF manuals can be found at the following URL:

http://publibz.boulder.ibm.com/cgi-bin/bookmgr_OS390/Shelves/ all13be9?filter=racf

IBM "redbooks" are another great online resource. These manuals derived their peculiar name long ago, when they were actually printed in book format. Their covers were always red, to distinguish them from other IBM publications. These days, the redbooks are available on CDs and also on the Internet.

The redbooks are different from other IBM manuals in that they are written by IBM specialists for specific important topics, or even for specific projects, such as how to handle a security conversion (or a migration). They present and discuss topics in easy-to-read tutorial format.

The main Internet link for all redbooks is at this URL:

http://publibz.boulder.ibm.com/cgi-bin/bookmgr_OS390/Shelves/REDB0304

If you are specifically looking for RACF and security redbooks, then the URL is as follows:

http://publibz.boulder.ibm.com/cgi-bin/bookmgr_OS390/Shelves/EZ33RA09

Get Free Utilities

The CBT "tape" is a collection of z/OS utilities, tools, and programs, all available for free. The programs have been written by various z/OS technical experts, over many years. The authors initially wrote the programs for their own use, no doubt, but they later contributed them to the CBT tape, in the hope that others would find them useful, too. The CBT tape got its name long ago, before the days of the Internet, when the programs were distributed on a physical tape cartridge. These days, of course, the tape is no longer available.

The CBT tape is available at the following URL:

http://www.cbttape.org/cbtdowns.htm

There are many useful RACF utilities available here. Just scan the index at the site. Of course, these programs are given out on an "as-is" basis, so you might need to do some work before you can use them at your installation.

Subscribe to Vendor Publications

Many vendor publications are free for the asking. Even if you simply browse through their pages, you will get a sense of what is happening in the mainframe security industry. One of the useful IBM publications, for example, is *IBM Systems Magazine*, available online at the following URL:

http://www.Ibmsystemsmag.com/mainframe

Use Native RACF Commands

Using the native RACF commands as much as you can is the best way to increase your RACF (and security) knowledge, for this tells you how the security system really works.

The downside is that some people find it hard to remember command syntax. While this might be true, there are important benefits. First, the commands will teach you a lot more than alternative means (for example, using ISPF panels) ever will. Second, RACF ISPF panels are cumbersome to use, and you might have to go through multiple panels before you accomplish a simple task. For this reason, some installations have not even bothered to implement RACF ISPF panels, even though they are free.

Learn DFSORT

The DFSORT utility does more than just sort data. You can also use it to select data from your RACF unload database. This capability can be very useful, as it allows you to produce simple reports using nothing more than DFSORT.

You can start out by using JCL to run simple DFSORT reports. DFSORT works well with data presented in a tabular format, such as that available in a RACF unload database.

For example, you can produce a quick report showing all RACF profiles that have universal access (UACC) higher than NONE, just by using DFSORT. For more information about the RACF unload database and examples of how to use DFSORT, refer to chapter 26.

Summary

IT training dollars are scarce these days. While improving your productivity is desirable, the resources to do so might simply not be there. For many security administrators, going to a conference such as SHARE or the Vanguard Security Conference is not a viable option. To make progress, you must find your own training resources. Hopefully, the methods in this chapter will help.

28

Security Compliance

*Most people spend more time and energy
going around problems than trying to solve them.*
—Henry Ford

In security terms, being compliant means you abide by various government and industry regulations. It also means you conform to your company's internal standards and practices. Your company should have information security standards that all users are expected to follow.

In addition, management must ensure that various external regulatory and compliance requirements are met. For example, the Sarbanes-Oxley (SOX) legislation was passed in the United States in 2002 after certain financial scandals came to light, such as the Enron debacle. Even though the legislation was passed only in the United States, most large companies across the globe are abiding by the intent of this legislation, whether voluntarily or because they are doing business with an American company and are therefore indirectly bound by SOX legislation.

Although the SOX legislation was passed because of a financial scandal, the effects of this legislation are felt in the information technology industry indirectly, since many of the financial transactions are done electronically.

Another outside regulatory standard that corporations, especially financial corporations, are expected to follow is the Payment Card Industry Data Security Standard, or PCI DSS. It applies to companies handling or processing cardholder information. PCI DSS is designed to reduce credit card fraud by requiring higher security standards for all such information.

When it comes to financial applications, internal and external auditors are very vigilant in making sure the company and its employees are compliant.

We mentioned SOX and PCI DSS. There might be others applicable to you, depending on the geographic location of your company. Whatever legislation may be in force at your organization, in general terms, your installation will be compliant if these mainframe security practices are observed:

1. There should be due diligence on management's part before granting or approving access to sensitive data.

2. Sensitive data (such as cardholder information or payroll records) must be identified so due diligence can be applied.

3. There should be periodic reviews of all access rights to sensitive information.

4. The company should implement the "segregation of duties" principle. This says that no single person should have multiple security powers, as this would potentially allow a person to perform unauthorized activities, and later hide his or her tracks.

✓ How Secure Is *Your* Installation?

Look at your DSMON report, discussed in chapter 2, "RACF Special Privileges." Do you see any user IDs with more than one special privilege? How about all three privileges? You should investigate those IDs to make sure they follow the principle of segregation of duties.

29

Security Best Practices

Men are only as good as their technical development allows them to be.
—George Orwell

Mainframe security has been around for quite some time. Over the years, installations have realized that some practices, if implemented, will pay security dividends in the long run. In fact, it can be argued that *not* establishing best practices and not following them is detrimental to overall security and often results in increased security administration costs.

With this in mind, this chapter presents some of the best practices for mainframe security.

Note: The best practices discussed in this chapter should not be treated in isolation from the rest of this book. Many of the ideas and suggestions mentioned elsewhere in this book are also industry best practices.

Implement Role-Based Security

In simple terms, role-based security is one where you grant access to groups instead of to individuals. Generally, these groups represent specific job functions at the company.

The employees' access rights are determined not by their user IDs being in the access lists, but by virtue of their being members of certain groups. If a group is in the access list, then the employee automatically will have access because he or she is a member of the group, as shown in Figure 29.1.

To administer security, you simply add and remove people from groups. The only time you have to modify the access list is when a new group is formed or when one is no longer needed.

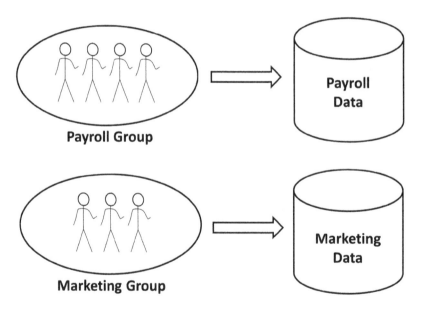

Figure 29.1: In role-based security, groups rather than individuals are in access lists.

There are several reasons why this model is appealing.

First, you will save on security administration costs. Under this scheme, groups, not individuals, will be in access lists. As people enter and leave various functional groups in your organization, you will not have to add and remove individuals from access lists.

Second, auditing will be easier. User IDs will be grouped according to their roles in the company, and the entire group, representing a role, will be granted access. To find out all users who have access to payroll data, for example, you simply list the group called "PAYROLL".

Last, it will help you in your user ID cloning efforts. Quite often, a request comes in to the security department such as "give the new employee Wayne the same access as that of Patricia." If you have implemented role-based security, all you have to do is list Patricia's user ID and find out what groups she is connected to. Then, you add Wayne to all these groups.

This simple cloning exercise would take much longer if you did not have role-based security. You would have to find out all profiles where Patricia has access, and also the level of that access (such as READ or UPDATE). There might be dozens, or even hundreds, of these profiles. You would then have to grant Wayne exactly the same level of access as Patricia to all these profiles.

Under role-based security, of course, a person is allowed to have more than one role. If that is the case, then that person simply belongs to more than one group.

So, under role-based security, are there any circumstances when you want to allow individual-level access? Yes, there are. Some access can rightly be granted at the individual level. This will happen when you have sensitive or critical data and you want to restrict it to just one or two individuals. In this case, granting access to entire groups would compromise the security of your important data.

When you adopt role-based security, one thing to keep in mind is group memberships. Since access is granted wholesale at the group level, it is assumed users are in the right groups. Otherwise, you are in a situation where the wrong people are getting access via incorrect group memberships.

Periodically De-Clutter Your Security Database

Database clutter is not very different from the physical clutter we collect in our basements and garages. It is an eyesore, gets in the way whenever we want to find something, and does not serve any useful function.

Security database clutter is bound to happen. Groups and user IDs become obsolete. Applications retire, requiring extensive cleanup of obsolete profiles. RACF groups become empty and might not be needed anymore. Employees transfer from one department to another. Departments get reorganized, and entire company divisions are bought and sold, not to mention mergers between companies.

You should regularly evaluate and make sure your security database is clutter-free. Otherwise, you will soon find yourself with a very large clutter that has accumulated and is now unmanageable.

Inactive user IDs should be reviewed and deleted where appropriate. The DSMON Selected User Attribute report shows all user IDs that have been revoked. For more information about this report, refer to chapter 3, "The Data Security Monitor (DSMON)."

Handle Employee Transfers and Terminations As They Occur

In any organization, people come and go. In some organizations, however, when people leave the company, their user IDs remain.

The security database cleanup associated with users being terminated or transferring to new job functions is often neglected. This neglect might go unnoticed for a long time.

There should be a process in place whereby the security department gets notified of all employee transfers and terminations.

If an employee moves on to a new job function, he or she will, over time, request the new access necessary to do the new job function. However, if you do not have a process in place to clean up his or her old access, then that old access will still remain intact.

This situation, if allowed to persist, will not only create the security database clutter mentioned above but will also cause security audit concerns, as the person does not need, and should not have, the old access any more. The problem is even worse in the case where the person held special security privileges in the old job.

In the case of employee terminations, make sure all access, and the user ID, is removed from the system. The concern here is that if the user ID inadvertently gets activated, then the access rights of that user ID are at risk of misuse.

Then there is the issue of what to do with the data sets owned by the person who has transferred or who has been terminated. These data sets cannot simply be deleted, as they might contain many years of work. In such cases, the best thing to do is to let the person's manager decide whether to reassign responsibility for the data or to delete it.

While cleanup activities such as these will not win you medals, or even recognition, they are a necessary evil. In the long run, it is in your best interest to keep things clean. Management should recognize this extra activity not as overhead, but as a job function within the security department.

Identify Your Important Data

There are two categories of data that can be designated as important:

- Critical operating system data (and its major components, such as DB2 and CICS)

- Your production data

While the first category is more or less standard across all companies and across all industries, the second category is installation-specific and therefore hard to identify. For example, for an automotive company, data sets containing auto part numbers and their specifications would be termed extremely critical to the business. There might well be legal reasons to guard this data from unauthorized access.

There are many benefits to identifying your important data:

- You can implement better security controls for this data.

- You can plan your disaster recovery exercises to include important data.

- The data owners and custodians will be better able to make access approval decisions.

- During access reviews, the owners will be able to make intelligent decisions.

- Auditors will know where to focus their audit efforts.

- Security administrators will be able to implement tighter controls and loggings for this data.

Assign Ownership to All Data

All data, especially the company's mission-critical data, must have an owner (or a custodian). Such a setup is useful in many ways:

- For access approval purposes, the security department knows where to go for approvals. The owners can make informed decisions, as they know their data the best.

- If there are discrepancies in access rights, then you can go to the owner for clarification purposes.

- The owner can make appropriate decisions about data backup requirements for recovery and disaster recovery purposes.

- Various compliance legislations require the company to have ownership of at least the production data.

Keep All Security Within RACF

In chapter 25, "Security Architecture," we see the benefits of having external security. In our case, this is RACF. It is recommended that, as far as possible, RACF be utilized as the security repository.

Some products provide the choice to implement either internal security or external security. Whenever there is a choice, it should be company policy to always select the latter.

There might be a few exceptions. Some applications, developed in-house or purchased from outside vendors, might offer only internal security. The application security requirements might be at the field level, and the whole process might be so customized that it makes sense to leave it up to the application group to manage their own security. This should be an exception rather than the rule, however.

Log Accesses to Important Data

The best practice of identifying all your important data was mentioned earlier in this chapter. If that is done, then implementing logging for important data is easy. These logs are invaluable for a number of reasons, among them the need to comply with corporate and regulatory standards.

Conduct Periodic Reviews of All Access Rights

A periodic review of all security definitions is essential to verify their continued applicability. This will give you a greater comfort level about your mainframe security.

For example, in the role-based security model discussed earlier in this chapter, members of a group automatically get certain access rights. It follows that if group membership is not periodically reviewed, then it is possible that wrong individuals have access to some data.

This activity is often overlooked, for the simple reason that it is not urgent, and the staff is busy doing daily security administration. To alleviate the workload on the security department, it is suggested that the review occur on a staggered basis.

Periodically—at least once a year—you should review the various pieces of information in the security database:

- Special privileges granted to user IDs

- All access rights

- User IDs

- Group memberships

- RACF profiles

Implement Change Management for Production JCL

Production JCL is what ultimately generates all those reports that are critical to the survival of corporations. Any changes, additions, or deletions to production JCL must go through a change management process whereby the JCL is examined before being put into production.

This JCL resides in one or more designated procedure libraries at the installation. Before it goes into production, make sure the following is true:

- The JCL has been tested. Otherwise, unexpected failures will affect the timely production of your critical reports.

- The JCL has been approved by management.

- The JCL runs under a production batch ID, and not a test ID or a personal user ID. If a personal user ID runs production JCL, what happens when the person leaves?

- The JCL does not reference any personal data sets. If it does, then changes made to the personal data sets can cause integrity issues. Also, what happens if the person leaves?

- The JCL follows corporate standards and naming conventions.

Report and Monitor Security Activities

In chapter 4, "Security Event Logging and Auditing," we saw the various logging capabilities that RACF provides and learned the importance of such logging. This logging is meaningless, however, unless you produce meaningful reports and monitor the security activities. (Of course, some logging is done for posterity, in case the need arises to find out what happened in the past.)

With regular monitoring, the security department becomes familiar with access patterns and is better able to fine-tune the security definitions that are in place. Also, if the user community is aware that monitoring is being done regularly, then there is less likelihood that someone will engage in fraudulent activity. It is like those traffic cameras randomly installed at key city intersections; just knowing that there might be one at the next intersection reduces the chances of motorists running red lights.

On a regular basis, you should produce reports and monitor the following:

- *Activities carried out by means of special privileges*—This includes all RACF security definition changes. This monitoring will ensure special powers are not abused.

- *Invalid logon attempts*—These are mostly a result of invalid passwords having been entered at logon time. You are looking for patterns that might tell you, for example, if someone is trying to use (or guess) someone else's password.

- *Security violations*—Inevitably, users try to access data they are not supposed to be accessing, and RACF fails the attempt. Even though the access attempt has failed, you should still keep an eye on these access violations to see if a pattern is emerging. For example, if you notice that a user ID is consistently failing on access attempts to your payroll master file, this should raise a red flag.

- *Accesses to important data*—In rare cases, for very important data, you might have set up logging even for successful accesses. These accesses need to be monitored to ensure the access was in line with the person's job function.

Implement Segregation of Duties

The principle of segregation of duties means that no individual should have multiple special privileges, such that the individual is able to carry out unauthorized activities and later cover his or her tracks by using special privileges.

In terms of job functions, segregation of duties implies that multiple sensitive functions should not be carried out by the same individual. For example, the person administering security by means of the RACF SPECIAL privilege should not also be the one to review the report on special privilege activities. These two functions should be segregated.

Require Approval Before Granting Access

When there is a request to grant access, the security department is in no position to make a judgment call as to whether the request is in line with company policy. Security administrators are the ones who should be granting the access, but only after the owner (or custodian) of that piece of data has approved the request. The owners are in the best position to make judgment calls on data they own.

Summary

If you adopt and implement security best practices at your organization, then the whole task of securing your company's business data becomes much easier. You will also be better prepared to meet with auditors and compliance monitors.

30

Security Add-On Products

If you reveal your secrets to the wind,
you should not blame the wind for revealing them to the trees.
—Kahlil Gibran

RACF is the primary provider of mainframe security. However, there are products in the market that enhance, or add on, to the functions provided by RACF.

By its sheer complexity, RACF cannot cater to all the needs of every security administrator. Some installations are eager to simplify the security administration function so that newcomers in the group can pick up the tasks without extensive training.

This void has created a market for the so-called RACF "add-on" products. These products add value to RACF by simplifying many of the daily RACF tasks and by providing functions not found in native RACF.

Typically, RACF add-on products are not marketed by IBM, but by third-party software vendors. Chief among these is Vanguard Integrity Professionals, with their Vanguard suite of products.

Most of the add-on products are ISPF-menu driven. And most of them work with a copy of the RACF database, usually taken the previous day. If they were to access the live RACF database, then response times would slow down.

The Benefits of RACF Add-On Products

RACF add-on products provide value to an organization by simplifying administration tasks and generally enhancing the security at the installation. When in-house knowledge is lacking, it is well worth acquiring these products. Even if they might appear to be expensive, they will pay for themselves in increased security and ease of security administration.

Newcomers to mainframe security are often big beneficiaries of these products. They do not have to learn native RACF commands, so they will be able to become productive much more quickly. Also, mistakes are less likely to occur when there is a friendly user interface.

As new features get introduced to RACF (or the z/OS operating system), these products keep pace with the changes, so you are assured of the benefits of the latest features.

In general, the main features of these products include the following:

- Simplified security administration

- Security monitoring

- Password resets

- Security reporting

- Security compliance and enforcement

Of course, not all products are alike, and not all provide all of these features, but since they're the most common, we'll look at them in more detail in the rest of this chapter.

Simplified Security Administration

Most add-on products focus on providing better security administration. This feature is often the deciding factor in the evaluation process.

They offer simplified methods to list user IDs, RACF groups, and profiles. Often, better masking and online panels are provided for this purpose. There are many examples, but the best one would be where you can list users based on the RACF "name" field, even by last name, if your installation's name field is set up that way. In addition, you can build bulk commands for later submission to RACF.

Another feature that appeals to customers is the "cloning" of user IDs, something you cannot do easily in native RACF. For example, the installation might get frequent requests along the lines of, "Give Mary the same access as Tom." Add-on products would do this very quickly.

Security Monitoring

These add-on products can continuously monitor the logs and trigger an alarm when predetermined security events occur. The trigger can be in the form of a generated email sent straight to the owner or person in charge of the affected resource. An example of a trigger would be an access violation to your payroll master file.

Invalid password attempts are typically harmless. However, if a pattern can be established, then "exception" reports can be generated for unusual password violations. Thus, you would see only potential intrusion attempts, and not the countless harmless violations.

Other areas of security monitoring include logs of profiles in WARNING mode and activities of user IDs having special privileges.

Password Resets

Add-on products often provide password reset capabilities. The resetting of passwords is usually automated via the Internet, after a few security verification questions are answered. This method is less error-prone than manual, human intervention.

Security Reporting

Security reporting in add-on products is usually user-friendly, and covers the gamut from profile listings to global settings.

Security Compliance and Enforcement

Security compliance and enforcement is achieved by the installation "telling" the add-on product what to enforce. Once this is set, the product will actually reject deviations from established standards and controls.

For example, if a user ID should not be changing SYS1.PARMLIB during the day (only a batch ID should do this), then this attempt will be prevented by the product, even though the person has access rights to the data set.

Summary

RACF add-on products are nice to have, but before you acquire them, you should justify their costs. In addition, you will need to evaluate your security requirements and then choose the product that best meets your needs.

Epilogue

Today this might seem far-fetched, but in the mid-1980s, the prevailing thought in some quarters was that the mainframes were going to be phased out. They would be replaced with those cheaper, simpler personal computers that were just making their mark. At the most, we were told, mainframes would survive another decade.

The proponents of this theory were usually the purveyors of personal computers themselves. They gave no thought to the security strengths of the mainframes, nor did they realize the security weaknesses in personal computers of those days.

Fast-forward 30 years, and we find nearly all large corporations—among them most Fortune 500 companies—still deploying mainframes as an integral part of their information technology strategy. And those mainframe installations still need strong security.

What happened?

The reason why mainframes are still around, and why they will be used for a long time to come, is best explained by an analogy: think of mainframes like giant trucks, requiring complicated maintenance, physical security, and a lot of money. Further, think of personal computers and midrange systems like wheelbarrows, which are nimble, quick to maneuver, easy to operate, and require little maintenance.

Wheelbarrows are initially much less expensive, but they introduce a host of issues. While large workloads in many cases can be distributed among many wheelbarrows, what do you do when you want to transport a giant, five-ton concrete slab? (Think of your client database, with tens of thousands of records.) The truck is ideal for this purpose, designed as it is to do such heavy work. The wheelbarrows, no matter how many you line up side-by-side, are ill-equipped to do the job. And how about the labor cost of individual operators, each one transporting a single wheelbarrow? Is it not better (and cheaper) to hire only one operator to drive the truck? Where do you store all these wheelbarrows, and how do you keep tabs on them to make sure they are not stolen?

No matter how you look at it, mainframes, and mainframe security, will continue to be here for a long, long time. This book was written with that in mind. It draws upon the personal and practical experiences I have accumulated over a long, fruitful, and enjoyable career in mainframe security. If it ignites in you even a small spark of interest in this vital topic, this book will have served its purpose.

Index